The Spiritual Writings of
Raphael Cardinal Merry del Val

The Spiritual Writings of Raphael Cardinal Merry del Val (1865–1930)

Edited, with an Introduction by
Harriet Murphy

GRACEWING

First published in 2009

Gracewing
2 Southern Avenue
Leominster
Herefordshire HR6 0QF

ISBN 978 0 85244 122 0

Typeset by Action Publishing Technology Ltd
Gloucester GL1 5SR

Contents

Introduction

Raphael Cardinal Merry del Val is best known to the world as the saintly Secretary of State to Pope St Pius X, who ruled the Church from 1903 to 1914. He was born at 33 Portman Square, London on 10 October 1865. This was the feast of the Jesuit, St Francis Borgia, whose name he received, when he was baptized the following day, along with many others, since his full name in Spanish is Rafael Maria José Pedro Francisco Borja Domingo Gerardo de la Santisma Trinidad Merry del Val y Zulueta. He was the second of four sons. His mother was Sofia Josefa de Zulueta, who died in 1925, the elder daughter of Pedro José de Zulueta, count of Torre Diaz, of the London bank of Zulueta and Company. Pedro's wife was Sophia Ann Wilcox, who was of Scottish and Dutch ancestry. The Zuluetas were an old Basque family, ennobled as counts de Torre Diaz in the nineteenth century. An English Zulueta called Canon Alfonso was a Jesuit who took over from Fr Ronald Knox as chaplain to Oxford University in 1939, later becoming parish priest of Our Most Holy Redeemeer in Chelsea.

Raphael's father was Rafael Merry del Val (1831–1917), the Marquis of Merry del Val, Secretary to the Spanish Legation in London, a monarchist supporter of King Alfonso XII, whose tutor he once was. The Marquis later became Ambassador to the court of Austro-Hungary and to the Holy See. The del Vals were an Aragonese family originally from Saragossa, claiming descent from a twelfth-century Breton crusader; the name Merry came from a line of Irish merchants from County

Waterford in Ireland who settled in the late eighteenth century in Seville. Cardinal Merry del Val's elder brother Alfonso, Marquis of Merry del Val, was born in 1864. He became Spanish ambassador to the Court of St James between 1913 and 1931. Cardinal Merry del Val's colourful ancestry entitles him to be called one of the 'English Cardinals', following a long line which includes such distinguished men in the Reformation and post-Reformation period as a canonized saint, St John Fisher; the son of a beatified martyr, Cardinal Reginald Pole, son of Blessed Margaret Pole; and a potential Doctor of the Church, the Venerable Cardinal Newman, whose cause is now advancing.[1]

Throughout his life, the Cardinal manifested the charisma of the Jesuits in his devotion to the Church Militant. Indeed, his enemies, following traditional anti-Catholic polemic, constantly referred to him as a puppet of that great Order which had so distinguished itself in the Counter-Reformation defending the Faith against heresy and error. Yet Cardinal Merry del Val was a worthy exponent of the Jesuit inheritance in the modern period. From 1907 he was associated with the Church's counter-Modernist crusade; indeed, his name is synonymous with it. Many still consider that the encyclical *Pascendi* (1907), which famously described Modernism as the 'synthesis of all heresies', was in part written by Pope St Pius X's brilliant Secretary of State.

In gratitude for the labours of the Jesuits at their school in Brussels (where young Raphael distinguished himself academically, as well as in music, drama and sports), the Cardinal offered up his First Mass at the Jesuit headquarters in Rome. This was on 1 January 1889 at the Gesù. Throughout his life his confessor was a Jesuit, Fr Celestino Alisiardi.

The new Father Raphael was incardinated in the Diocese of Westminster, and the country of his birth never lost its significance for him. He was blessed with a great desire to suffer for

---

[1]   See G. C. Heseltine, *The English Cardinals* with some account of those of other English-speaking countries (London: Burns, Oates and Washborne, 1931), and Fr Nicholas Schofield and Fr Gerard Skinner, *The English Cardinals,* with a foreword by Cardinal Cormac Murphy-O'Connor (Oxford: Family Publications, 2007).

the conversion of England, where he made his first Holy Communion on 29 August 1875. England also educated him. He attended Bayliss House in Berkshire, Remington's in Hampshire, and Ushaw College. In fact, his devotion to England was so great, he positively protested when Pope Leo XIII expressed his desire to reserve him for the Vatican.

In a letter from Vienna dated 25 October 1890 to a priest-friend at the Birmingham Oratory, Fr Denis Sheil, he mentions his exam in Theology and his defence of the Immaculate Conception, which had been extremely demanding. 'The six hours were not sufficient to finish it in,' he said. He was examined orally by a Jesuit, the then Fr Billot, who kept him 'under torture' on the same thesis. But in the same letter he also makes a passing reference to a communication to the Pope, begging him to be released from public life so that he could go on the missions. He was, we assume, not enamoured of the intense world of college, university and Vatican life which he had sampled thus far in Rome. He was only twenty-five. In another anguished letter of 18 December 1901, eleven years later, the issue of his residing in the Vatican was still a burning one. As President of the Ecclesiastical Academy in Piazza Minerva, he begged the reigning pontiff to relieve him of his grand duties, offering himself as an ordinary parish priest to minister to English-speaking souls in Rome. His request was not granted. The Pope had other ambitions. Cardinal Merry del Val, his protégé, spoke and wrote faultless Latin, English, Spanish, French and Italian. He was from a diplomatic, cosmopolitan and aristocratic background, with Spanish, Irish, Dutch and English blood. His studies at the Gregorian and the Accademia dei Nobili Ecclesiastici, which ended in 1891, had given him qualifications in Theology, Philosophy and Canon Law. He was clearly brilliant. He was even modern. He used typewriters, telephones, elevators and cars, to the consternation of the anti-moderns. All this for the greater glory of God.

Did the humiliation of not getting his own way mean he played no part in preparing the way for the conversion of England? Clearly not. He is known to have written the famous prayer for the conversion of England, usually recited at Benediction, which Pope Leo XIII included in his encyclical to the English people *Amantissima Voluntatis* (1895), and which remains the best known and best loved of his own prayers, reproduced in this volume. Moreover, in 1896 he was secretary to the commission that investigated the validity of Anglican Orders, declaring them 'null and void', thus paving the way for many converts, of whom Merry del Val received at least forty into the Church. His private correspondence from that period proves that he was absolutely indispensable in informing the Pope about the complicated aspects of the break with Rome in English Reformation history. He was instrumental in preventing the more liberal inclinations of Cardinals Rampolla and Gasparri – influenced by Modernist priests like Abbé Portal and Abbé Duchesne as well as Protestants in favour of Anglo-Catholic hegemony, like Lord Halifax – from delivering the wrong verdict simply for the sake of ending the schism. Cardinal Gasparri had taught at the 'Institut Catholique' in Paris before returning to Rome, and actually published a monograph in favour of the Church recognizing Anglican Orders in 1896. Yet Cardinal Merry del Val was particularly suspicious of Cardinals Gasparri and Rampolla with regard to the question of Anglican Orders, saying in one astonishing letter that he did not know where Cardinal Gasparri 'had learnt or unlearnt his Theology'. Here we glimpse Merry del Val's impatience with those who did not share his gift of penetrating judgement, angry at the way Cardinals Rampolla and Gasparri were united in what he felt was an excessive enthusiasm to end the schism in England, which in part caused them to underestimate the doctrinal obstacles. That is the most charitable gloss that one can put on the irate references of Merry del Val to their positive overtures to the schismatics. So Merry del Val was clearly an instrument of Divine Providence in the Vatican over the question of Anglican Orders, since he alone, as an Englishman with years of experience living in England, seems to have understood how un-Catholic English Protestantism was in 1896. He played an absolutely pivotal role in ensuring that Pope Leo XIII was not led astray by the false arguments of the Liberalisers who had his ear.[2]

---

[2]   See Harriet Murphy, 'Cardinal Merry del Val and the Conversion of England: Part I', *Christian Order*, December 2006, and Harriet Murphy, 'Cardinal Merry del Val and the Conversion of England: Part II', *Christian Order*, January 2007.

Anglican Orders were not declared 'null and void' but *'absolutely* null and void'. Why so? Because of a defect of form in the Edwardine Ordinal used by Anglicans since the Reformation to confer Holy Orders – the words were not intended to mean what the Church had always meant by the sacrament of Holy Orders – and a defect of intention in the consecrating bishops and clergy – who likewise did not believe in a sacrificing priesthood, transubstantiation or the Mass as a propitiatory sacrifice for the expiation of sins and for the relief of the holy souls in Purgatory. Work on this historic judgment brought Merry del Val into contact with Cardinal Gasquet, Abbot of Downside, and Cardinals Bourne and Vaughan, Archbishops of Westminster, all of whom became staunch allies and supporters in defence of the Catholic Church in England. Indeed, the vital private corre-spondence between Cardinal Gasquet and Cardinal Merry del Val is still kept in Downside's archives, and it tracks the progress of the work being done, right up to the day of the publication of the ruling. In his apologetic work in defence of the judgment against Anglican Orders, Cardinal Merry del Val made the following unequivocal statement in a letter to his friend, Fr Woodlock SJ, on 16 January 1930.

> If a minister uses a valid form, it is most difficult, often impos-sible, to prove that his personal intention invalidated the sacra-ment, unless clear evidence is forthcoming and absolutely inconclusive. But that is not the point here. If a minister uses a corrupt or mutilated form, the intention is expressed in the rite itself, viz. the intention of excluding the definite object and effect of the Sacrament.

On that basis, the Cardinal notes that all with Anglican Orders do not have doubtful orders, but invalid orders. For that reason if Anglican vicars received into the Church wanted to proceed to holy orders and become Catholic priests, they were not 'condi-tionally' ordained, but 'unconditionally' ordained. He then went on to clarify that the judgment was an infallible one.

> The Cardinals were unanimous in declaring the Orders absolutely invalid. The Holy Father took further time to consider

the matter and then drew up his dogmatic Bull, concerning a dogmatic fact, thereby involving indirectly if not directly his infallibility; for if with a given form before his eyes he cannot decide whether or not it contains the essential elements of a valid sacrament, what becomes of his infallibility?[3]

Elsewhere on 28 July 1925, the Cardinal mentioned in a letter to Fr Woodlock that Pope Leo XIII intended the decision to be 'irreformable for all time'.[4]

Cardinal Merry del Val also helped write the 'Letter of Our Holy Father by Divine Providence Pope Leo XIII to the Bishops of England' in 1899. This expressed the Holy Father's gratitude for the work of the Bishops for the conversion of England in the wake of the condemnation of Anglican Orders. Then, in 1908 the Cardinal was instrumental in lifting the slur on the English-born recusant nun, Mary Ward, who founded the Institute of the Blessed Virgin Mary, recently renamed as the Congregatio Jesu, for which the Institute has always been grateful. The cordial relations between both are symbolized by the gift of a most beautiful image of Our Lady of Perpetual Succour from the Cardinal, which the nuns keep in their house in Cambridge, England. He was their Lord Protector for a while. For the last year of his life he was Lord Protector of the Beda College in Rome, whose constitutions he helped to create, modeled on the priestly confraternity founded by St Philip Neri. This brought to completion the revival of the Beda, which had been a slow process, begun in the reign of Blessed Pio Nono when the hierarchy was restored in England in 1850. The Cardinal also ministered to the English-speaking community at St Silvestro's, to this day popular with English-speaking peoples in Rome. He played tennis and billiards at the North American College. He helped the English-speaking nuns of the Poor Servants of the Mother of God – founded by Mother Magdalen Taylor, a convert (1832–1900) – who are still living in the street just off Piazza di Spagna where Cardinal Merry del Val used to visit them.

---

[3] Letter in the Jesuit Archives, Farm Street.
[4] Letter in the Jesuit Archives, Farm Street.

He knew the Blue Nuns at Calvary Hospital. They had been founded by the English woman, Venerable Mother Mary Potter, to assist the sick at the moment of death. They no longer run the hospital, and the nuns and the body of Venerable Mother Mary are now in Nottingham. For seven years, from 1893 to 1900, he was their ordinary confessor. He was Lord Protector of the Josephites, who are associated with St George's, Weybridge. Merry del Val also lived to see the beatification of the forty martyrs of England and Wales in 1929, another significant moment in the emergence of England's true national character after centuries of recusant Catholicism, anti-Catholic laws and Catholic life without a hierarchy.

He was also instrumental in defusing another crisis in English Catholicism – the problems associated with ecumenism. These issues were becoming pressing concerns in the 1920s as the general public was confused by the obvious battles between militant apologists for a union of Catholicism and Anglo-Catholicism which did not entail conversion, and those who insisted that Anglo-Catholics had to *submit to Rome*. His friendship with the Jesuit Fr Woodlock at Farm Street meant the two fought together to dispel the effects of the Malines conversations. These conversations in Belgium involved Lord Halifax and Cardinal Mercier. Cardinal Merry del Val acted as Fr Woodlock's adviser, as we have seen above. Fr Woodlock took it upon himself to be the antagonist of the ecumenically inclined, in a series of articles in the press. We wonder what both would think of the by now standard laments about the 'shame' of the Church's condemnation of Anglican Orders amongst the ecumenical confraternity; we also wonder what both would think of the largest ever Vatican delegation attending the Lambeth Conference in 2008, where Fr Timothy Radcliffe, OP, and Cardinal Walter Kasper joined Cardinal Murphy-O'Connor in hoping to help the Archbishop of Canterbury 'save' the Anglican Communion at a time when its internal divisions have multiplied since the famous Lambeth Conference in 1930, at which the real unity between true Christians world wide was first rent asunder. We allude to the landmark approval of contraception within marriage made by Lambeth, which shocked the world and began the rapid descent into absolute equivocation which has resulted in the public promotion of contraception, divorce, remarriage, abortion and sodomy, and the near complete disappearance of Christian morality. Together with the ordination of women to orders which the Catholic Church has never recognized anyway, the contemporary, outright rejection of the scriptural foundations for basic Christian doctrines and morality raises questions as to what the Vatican expects to gain and what the Vatican expects the general public to make of the apparent equivocation over the absolute terms of *Dominus Jesu* (2000).

What else did Cardinal Merry del Val do for England? He spoke at a very significant diplomatic event in the crypt of St Peter's Basilica in Rome, when on 6 February 1925 a commemorative plaque was hung above the tomb of the only English Pope, Hadrian/Adrian IV, who died in 1159. Before Hadrian became Pope he had, as Nicholas Breakespear, acted as a legate. He had been dispatched by Pope Eugene III to Norway on a diplomatic mission to solve a delicate crisis. In 1925 the Norwegian government had contacted the Pope for permission to commemorate this mission. The ceremony in the crypt of St Peter's was presided over by the Cardinal, then Archpriest of the Basilica. He promptly practised the kind of ecumenism of which the Church has always approved. Cardinal Merry del Val said, quite simply, in the presence of the non-Catholic Ambassador of Norway, that he longed for an end to all that the Reformation had done to destroy truth and beauty, which he believed could only be guaranteed by the See of Peter. These were unequivocal words.

Finally, the Cardinal is also still remembered very affectionately at Ushaw College, Durham, where a 'Merry del Val' tree is regularly watered in his honour. It was planted there by the great man himself on a return visit to his Alma Mater, on 25 August 1907. As if to reinforce all of his devotion to England, his tomb in the crypt of St Peter's is right next to that of James III, Henry, Cardinal Duke of York and Prince Charles Edward. Perhaps their proximity points to the triumph of the Immaculate Heart of Mary and the conversion of

England, for which there is proof in a number of prophecies and in the devotion of countless English souls since the Reformation to that very cause.

For some of these reasons the Cardinal has always had a great following in the English-speaking world. The Legion of Merry del Val in England – founded by Miss Joan de Trafford in 1965 – has always promoted knowledge of him and has attempted to promote the cause, as has the more recent Merry del Val Society, founded in England by Miss Julia Callaghan in 1986. Englishman and Catholic apologist Robin Anderson, who died in Rome in 2005, devoted his life to the Church working for Vatican Radio. Living in Rome, he was for years a semi-official promoter of the Cardinal's cause. As the name 'Legion' shows, Merry del Val had become linked with the battle in defence of the Faith. Indeed, after the Second Vatican Council, veteran priest Fr Noel Barbara founded an institute in Tours, France to defend the Faith against the heresy of Modernism. He named it after the Cardinal for the simple reason that the Cardinal's name was synonymous with intransigence in all matters of faith and morals.

Finally, because of the Cardinal's Spanish ancestry, he has also always had a strong following in the Spanish-speaking world. He was, for a time, Lord Protector of the Pontifical Spanish College, Rome, a college he helped to found along with Blessed Manuel Domingo y Sol in 1892, who regarded his mentor as an angel, forever grateful for opening so many doors for him in the Vatican. Merry del Val celebrated his second Mass at the Spanish church near the Quirinale, run by the Trinitarian order, mostly of Spanish origin. He was consecrated Archbishop in a church linked to the national Marian shrine of Spain, of Monserrat. That church in Rome is called Santa Maria in Monserrato degli Spagnoli. The Spanish people effectively provided the funds for the new tomb for the Cardinal in the crypt of St Peter's, with sumptuous stone from Majorca, which was inaugurated on 11 January 1931. Indeed, the Spanish College now has all the documents relating to the Cardinal's cause for beatification, his private altar and some of the relics from the altar, his penitential instruments, his old bed, a statue of the Curé d'Ars, and a number of portraits, including one he commissioned of the 'Addolorata', and a painting of a Spanish ancestor, the child saint Dominguito del Val, who was crucified by the Jews on Good Friday in Saragossa Cathedral in Spain. For this reason the Cardinal always had a particular devotion to the cause of the conversion of the Jews.[5]

The current postulator, Mgr Tomás-Amable Díez Olano, who is Spanish, lives in the Spanish College where the cause sleeps for want of interest and money.

The Birmingham Oratory priest Fr Denis Sheil and the Cardinal had both been students together at the Scots College, Rome. Both remained in close contact throughout the Cardinal's life, Fr Sheil visiting him in Rome once a year to keep his friend company. This is why Fr Sheil's knowledge of the great man's character is so indispensable. At the trial which opened the Cardinal's cause in Rome in 1953, Fr Sheil stated that his friend embraced his high rank and duties in an exemplary fashion, accepting both as a cross which went against his heart's desire. Fr Sheil said the following:

> I occupied a very special position in regard to the Servant of God. We were not only most intimate friends but he made me his confidante and all through the years of stress wrote frequently, unveiling his heart. I therefore think it my duty *ad testis de visu* to record the Servant of God's interior dispositions throughout his brilliant career, namely his complete detachment from all honours and a longing for Apostolic work in the obscurity of parochial life. God's special Providence thrust upon him a life long cross. First in the incredible action of Pope Leo in sending him to the Accademia against his own father's will and in spite of the Servant of God's repugnance, and secondly the untoward death of Monsignor Volpini, which was the direct cause of coming into contact with Blessed Pius X.

---

[5]   The founder of modern Zionism, Theodor Herzl, met with Pope St Pius X in a historic audience, arranged by Cardinal Merry del Val, on the feast of the Conversion of St Paul, 1904. But the Pope said that he could not bestow his blessing on the movement to give the Jews a homeland in what is now Israel, because they had rejected Christ and did not accept His divinity.

This has been corroborated independently. In a letter to his priest-friend Fr Joey Broadhead from Ushaw dated 29 October 1903, he says about his new honour as Secretary of State that 'it is a death sentence'. In another, to the American Monsignor O'Connell dated 9 May 1901, concerning his friend's nomination as bishop of Portland and the social festivities attached to that, he says: 'You will let me off dinners and invitations of that kind, won't you? That is the part which does not matter and which I like to avoid.'

So what more can be said about the Cardinal's exceptional life as Secretary of State to the last pope to be canonized? And who was the patron of that most famous first encounter between Merry del Val and Cardinal Giuseppe Sarto? The answer is Our Lady of Good Counsel, whose shrine is kept in Genazzano, south of Rome, where the miraculous image remains a symbol of our Lady's desire to protect Christendom from Christ's enemies, then as now. It is a site of pilgrimage which has always been popular with reigning pontiffs on account of its proximity to Rome, and has a special liturgical feast day on 25 April. Merry del Val, who was then only a titular archbishop of Nicea and not even a cardinal, was secretary of the conclave which assembled in Rome at the death of Pope Leo XIII in 1903 to elect the new Pope.[6] Merry del Val had been commissioned to go and rescue poor old Sarto, who was already emerging as the preferred candidate, from the Sistine chapel. The great Cardinal was praying in front of an image of Our Lady of Good Counsel. The two had only met the day before the conclave began, on 3 August 1903. Sarto had no desire to reign as Pope. In the Sistine Chapel his 'tears were streaming from his eyes', according to Merry del Val's account. Was he going to resist his candidature or agree? Merry del Val intervened to tell him: 'Eminence, take courage, our Lord will help you'. Our Lady of Good Counsel, before whom they both knelt, thus saw that Sarto was given good counsel by the thirty-eight-year-old Archbishop. Sarto agreed to be the preferred candidate. The next day he obtained

[6] See Harriet Murphy, 'An Open Question finally resolved: The 1903 Conclave', *Christian Order*, November 2007.

the necessary votes. Sarto became Pope Pius X, and the rest is history.

The relationship which Pope St Pius X had as Pope with his Secretary of State was not only an exceptional one, but an exceptionally moving one, united as they both were in a deep love of Holy Mother Church, both ready to suffer for that great cause. Testimonies show that the relationship was both formal and informal. The Pope used to quip, for instance, that the press had stylized him as no more than a dim-witted son of a peasant farmer. The press liked to see his Secretary of State as a young pipsqueak and upstart, a malevolent force able to take advantage of the unsophisticated ways of his peasant boss. The truth is that Merry del Val's devotion to his master was most apparent in his determination to defend his prerogatives as Pope and Vicar of Christ. But it was also intensely personal. In a letter written shortly after Pope St Pius X's death, dated 27 September 1914, the Cardinal said to his 'dear old friend' Fr Joey Broadhead:

> The blow has been a terrible one for me, and my heart is fairly broken. You see, I loved Pius X with every fibre of my soul: He was more than a father to me, and I feel as if I could not live without him. He was indeed a saint.

This has not prevented speculative historiography from continually alleging that Cardinal Merry del Val was a tyrant, who even had the Pope under his thumb; nor has it prevented historians from stylizing the Pope as weak and vacillating in the face of the Cardinal's stronger will, the victim of his 'aristocratic' superiority complex.

Both these tendencies point to a blind spot about the Church Militant, particularly prevalent among liberal Catholics or those who are outside the Church. They perhaps do not understand that the Church is not a human body, but is rather divinely instituted with rights that no human authority or power can usurp, the 'Mystical Body of Christ'. As the Mystical Body of Christ the Church is without sin, error or defect. Logically, therefore, Her rights and prerogatives have always been under attack by those who would prefer the Church to be on an equal footing with other religions and other sects, and who resent the Church's exclusive claims. Cardinal Merry del Val was a valiant member of the Church Militant inasmuch as he was a great defender of the Faith against errors and heresies, and of Her rights as a divine body, instituted by our Lord Jesus Christ, and the revealed truth *extra ecclesiam nulla salus*. He always knew of the intensity of the hatred of Holy Mother Church, especially the rebukes administered to Her by secular powers, not least because he experienced them at first hand. This explains why, in his own lifetime, he was frequently stylized by the press as the 'grand Inquisitor', the 'Torquemada' of modern times, the intransigent and intolerant devotee of integral Catholicism capable of taking on France, President F. D. Roosevelt, the Jewish head of civic Rome, Nathan, and the Masons, when they presumed to treat the Church as a sect. The latter group venerated the heretic Giordano Bruno beneath the eyes of the Vatican even in Pope St Pius X's days, which the Pope and his Secretary of State rightly saw as an unwarranted and unnecessary provocation. On one of Giordano Bruno's anniversaries, the Masons succeeded in upsetting the young St Maximilian Kolbe. On 16 October 1917 his 'Militia' of the Immaculate was formed in Rome as a proximate response to this kind of provocation, the only possible counter-force to organized evil which did not blush to raise its ugly head in Vatican City itself. Merry del Val did not take on the Masons to provoke, but rather to defend, for which he earned their contempt.

So it is edifying to know that he led a simple life, going about his business in great faith, hope and charity, confident that Almighty God would see to it that truth would triumph. He reserved much of his torment and anguish for private correspondence. In a letter to Fr Broadhead dated 19 September 1907, Merry del Val states in no uncertain terms how powerful the Vatican's antagonists are in their quest to de-christianize the world. He says that they hate him in France in particular. This was because he did everything in his power to protect the rights of Holy Mother Church when they tried to end the Napoleonic Concordat, illegally declaring the separation of the Church from the State in 1905, closing down churches, confiscating church property, forcing the orders into exile, making life for Catholics at every level exceptionally difficult. In the contest between divine love and diabolical hatred of the truth, Cardinal Merry del Val knew he was nothing more than a target for the frustrations of the enemy, given his ability to condemn these illegalities in the name of peace and in the name of true justice. The letter reads: 'the international lodges who are working for secularism cannot forgive me the stand in France, which has prevented them from carrying out their general plan of destruction of religion'.

The Cardinal believed so strongly in the Church Militant that he was in either single or double figures for the papacy in the conclave which finally elected Pope Pius XI in 1922, at the death of Pope Benedict XV. The facts vary according to the accounts one reads. That he was a candidate was in part due to his reputation as the brilliant Secretary of State of Pope St Pius X, and his staunch defence of the orthodox Faith against the heresy of Modernism.[7] He became the candidate for the 'intransigent' constituency only because of the proximate danger of a weaker, more liberal cardinal being given control of the whole Church. This was not because he was ambitious, as his opponents like to allege, but rather because he saw it as his duty to save the Church from the enemies within. Once again, there are rumours and speculative theories still in circulation as to what exactly went on in that particular conclave in 1922. We know that Cardinal Gasparri and Cardinal Merry del Val did not see eye to eye, as we have already indicated in the question of Anglican Orders. Cardinal Gasparri is responsible for circulating the rumour that Cardinal Merry del Val was motivated by nothing other than raw ambition at the conclave.

Cardinal Gasparri was, at the time, the preferred candidate of France, where he had been popular when teaching Canon Law at the Institut Catholique in Paris. The French government presumably saw in him a man who would allow them to hold on to their gains against the Church, since the separation

---

[7]   See Shane Leslie, *Cardinal Gasquet: A Memoir* (London: Burns & Oates, 1953), p. 253.

from the State had come into effect in 1905, and was still working against the best interests of the Church, with Catholics still the object of public contempt and even persecution, their right to exist openly called into question by such acts as the pillaging and unlawful seizure of church property and the restrictions placed upon the association of the laity with the clergy. Since the Masons in France, as we have seen, never forgave Cardinal Merry del Val for condemning the French government's actions in 1905, it is not surprising they had no desire to see him elected reigning pontiff. The fact that France viewed Gasparri as an attractive candidate certainly implies that Masonic France expected to get more concessions from the Vatican through Gasparri, or at least the maintenance of the status quo, which they would arguably not have got with Cardinal Merry del Val as pope. Was the French government happy with the result of the 1922 conclave when they did not get Gasparri as Pope but Pope Pius XI, with Gasparri remaining as Secretary of State? It would seem so, but is there any supporting evidence elsewhere?

The historical record confirms that Masonic France benefited from this new alliance with Gasparri, since Gasparri and Pope Pius XI went on to condemn Action Française in 1926. This was the single most powerful body of opposition to the French government, and it was composed largely of monarchists, traditionalists, integral and intransigent Catholics. It had a unified voice and excellent, adversarial journalism of the first order under the leadership of the great Charles Maurras. The group was even capable of bringing down the government, of mobilizing opposition on the streets, and was thus more than the proverbial thorn in the side of the government. That condemnation did not, apparently, enjoy the approval of all the Cardinals – although this is yet another controversial area of disagreement with endless rumour – and led to Cardinal Billot offering the first-ever resignation of a Cardinal, an unheard of act, in protest at the Vatican's imprudence and injustice. In the sense that the Pope and his Secretary of State were acting at the behest of an unrepresentative clique in the French bishops' conference, the condemnation has some 'authority', although it is not beyond the realm of possibility that internal sabotage was at work. One is justified in asking questions about the judgement of the Roman pontiff and his Secretary of State on this political matter, which is not protected by infallibility by definition. The facts are plain. The Vatican condemnation was a gift to Masonry in France and it liquidated, in one fell swoop, intelligent, passionate, organized, Catholic opposition to Masonry's plot to destroy the Church and Catholicism. At the same time, the genius of the Church was such that an alternative plan continued to subvert the conspiracies of the enemies. In his encyclical *Custodi di quella Fede* on Free Masonry, of 8 December 1892, Pope Leo XIII had called on the laity to form associations under the influence of priests. This project came to be known as Catholic Action and flourished, especially after Pope St Pius X's *Il Fermo Proposito* of 1905 on the same topic, which had been preceded by a *motu proprio* in 1903 reiterating the duties of lay members of the Church.

It is interesting to note that Cardinal Gasparri also played a successful role in liquidating Fr Luigi Sturzo, who had an equivalent function in Italian life and politics in the same period. He had founded the Partito Popolare Italiano in the 1920s, and was doing great works throughout the country to ensure Christian standards in politics and public life, educating the electorate in their knowledge of how to reconcile Christianity with democracy, trying to win arguments rationally and to gain support for a reform of the electoral system to favour what we would call the principle of 'subsidiarity', local government for the people and in the people's interests. He was a rare bird, someone who could combine theory with practice, who was welcomed by the English hierarchy when he went into exile in England. He was also an eloquent speaker and writer, and an academic. The Church remained wary of this orator-politician priest, and in this period tightened up its discipline, making it more than just not licit for a priest to be politically active. Fr Romolo Murri, for instance, had been a more brutally 'engaged' kind of priest-politician, and had been excommunicated by Pope St Pius X for refusing to give up his political life. Yet Fr Sturzo was obviously different, and hardly susceptible to Modernism in the political sphere as other priests may have been. He was a very pious priest, who never claimed to be anything other than a priest, working in the name of the Church to establish the reign of Christ on earth. Nonetheless, Cardinal Gasparri, on the orders of Pope Benedict XV, asked Fr Sturzo, on the strength of the convention that priests are not supposed to be politically active, to desist and to withdraw from public life in Italy. Fr Sturzo agreed to obey, and went into exile in North America and London, and never returned to active political life. Very well regarded as a sociologist in a truly Catholic sense, Fr Sturzo's cause has recently been opened. It is a matter of conjecture what might have happened in Italy if he had continued with his adversarial journalism, writing and public speaking, confronting the Italian people with the real obstacles to peace in the world, namely Masonry and its satellite organizations. He united Catholics in a front against a common enemy, but without appealing to their base instincts.

It also still remains a matter of speculation what the Church might have done had Cardinal Merry del Val been made Pope in 1922. It is interesting in this context to read of his own verdict on the Church after the death of Pope St Pius X. In one of his letters of the period he said the Church was 'drifting'. It is possible, according to the sources, that he saw the advances of militant atheism under Communism as the greatest threat to the survival of the Faith on earth. He was already warning the West about militant atheism in 1933. It is said that Cardinal Merry del Val was preparing a tract against Communism towards the end of his life. Does this chime in with the apparition of our Blessed Lady in Fatima in 1917, where our Lady famously singled out Russia, saying Russia would spread errors throughout the world if the pope did not consecrate Russia to the Immaculate Heart of Mary? Was the reference to Russia a recognition of the full force of militant atheism in Communism, which had successfully toppled theocratic monarchy at exactly the same time?

Cardinal Merry del Val led a penitential, hidden life. He was a great director of souls, spending hours in the confessional, preaching retreats, receiving over forty converts into the Church in the period 1894–1904, and visiting his beloved boys in Trastevere, in the Sacred Heart Association which he had founded in

1889 for the destitute, for social outcasts and for the protection and nurturing of souls. Whenever relieved from the great burdens of his post as Secretary of State to Pope St Pius X, he loved to visit the boys. In order to be enrolled in the association, the boys had to be between twelve and twenty years old. The purpose of the pious association was to make reparation for sacrilege in honour of the Sacred Heart. Members were expected to wear the brown scapular, say the rosary, set a good example, honour the Sacred Heart on the special feast days, have holy water in their bedrooms and so on. It is thought that at times there were as many as 200 in the association. On his visits to Trastevere the Cardinal used to supervise the boys in their recreation, and permitted them all sorts of games and sports, and theatre. The amateur dramatics were attended by the Pope's pious sisters, by professors at the University, and were considered to be of a high standard. The testimonies of the boys are an astonishing record of the esteem in which the Cardinal was held. The protection offered by so august a figure as the Cardinal meant that the apostolate resulted in many religious vocations. Cardinal Ottaviani was one of them. The association is still in existence today, and there is a street in Trastevere named after the Cardinal in honour of the association. We include in this volume the Cardinal's beautiful poem to the Sacred Heart, which demonstrates how deeply felt his love was for this great, Catholic devotion. The Cardinal was also instrumental in spreading devotion to the Sacred Heart as confessor to the Sacred Heart nuns at Trinità dei Monti, headquarters of the congregation founded by the French woman St Madeleine Sophie Barat, some of whose relics Cardinal Merry del Val had on his private altar.

Raphael Merry del Val was in great demand in the Via Lucchesi with the Sisters of Maria Riparatrice, founded by the Belgian aristocrat, Blessed Emilie D'Oultremont (1818–1878). He was regularly at their disposal from 1893 to 1903. One of the depositions by Anna Elisabetta (née Bell) states that in 1902 she went to the sisters there every day for two whole months to be instructed in the doctrines of the Faith, when she, as a Protestant was preparing to marry a Catholic. Have times changed, or is this still the case? The Cardinal was also Lord Protector of a congregation founded by the Spaniard, Blessed Dolores R.

Sopena (1848–1918), which was devoted to teaching the cate-chism. There are seventy-nine letters to members of the congre-gation alone among the papers kept at the Spanish College and the relations were close, not least because the nuns from this congregation kept his apartment clean! Their apostolate was very unconventional for the day, given that they wore civilian clothing, the better to be able to reach out to souls in need of the catechism. Pope St Pius X was delighted to give them his appro-bation, since instructing souls in the Faith was seen as the best antidote to Modernism.

It would be impossible to do justice to the extent and range of the Cardinal's commitments throughout Rome, but a letter to a family member dated 19 March 1926 says that he had by that date ordained a total of 265 priests at the Spanish College alone. He also co-consecrated the Bishop of Treviso and the Bishop of Rieti, both of whose causes have been entered. Blessed Andrea Giacinto Longhin (1863–1936), a Cappuchin, was a staunch anti-Modernist bishop of Treviso. Venerable Massimo Rinaldi (1869–1941) was a member of the missionary congregation founded by Blessed John Scalabrini and wrote the most perfect exhortations in faultless Italian, inspiring many souls to perse-vere in the spiritual life.

The historical record seems to be complete. The Vatican finished cataloguing the Cardinal's private library in 2006. His papers as Secretary of State are available to the general public in the Vatican Secret Archives. Countless university libraries and diocesan archives throughout Europe and North America, in Boston, Durham, St Andrews, Paris and London also have important documents. Many of them were originally photo-copied and sent to Rome when the cause was opened in the same year the Church canonized Pope St Pius X, so they can also be consulted at the Spanish College. Yet we also need to fill in the picture of his activities in a public capacity once Pope St Pius X died. After 1914, until his death in 1930, the Cardinal was Secre-tary of the Congregation of the Doctrine of the Faith – the post most recently occupied by the then Cardinal Ratzinger – while also still holding other important posts at the Vatican. We hope that in future years scholars will be able to consult the papers from the period after the death of the Pope. We also hope that access to the catalogue of the private library will lead to some new insights, since these papers were not available to the first archivist in 1933, Pio Cenci, whose extensive work is still the basis for all the biographies of the Cardinal still in circulation. Meanwhile, we owe an enormous debt to the present scholar at the Secret Vatican Archives, Alejandro Dieguez, whose detailed inventory of many of Pope St Pius X's papers can now be used to fill in more of the lesser-known details of his pontificate.[8]

There is, meanwhile, fierce opposition to the Cardinal's cause from France to this day, on account of the Cardinal's response to the French government's unilateral separation of the Church from the State in 1905, ruining all the good work Pope Leo XIII had done to rally French Catholics to the government for the sake of their common goals. In addition, academic historians of a liberal persuasion are still circulating this caricature of the Cardinal as the wicked Inquisitor, an image that the international press indulged freely in his lifetime, causing Pope St Pius X endless anguish. Cardinal Merry del Val is thus arguably being instrumentalized in subversive historiography of the Church by those who are either open Modernists, or crypto-Modernists. A perfect example is Lawrence Barman's study of Baron Friedrich von Hügel's implication in Modernism. Barman talks about Pope St Pius X and Cardinal Merry del Val as if they were the guilty ones, not the Modernists. The Cardinal and his boss were apparently practitioners of something he calls with contempt 'extreme ultramontanism'.[9]

Two instances will suffice to prove that he had no acrimony with respect to anyone, and no purely personal hatred of those who did not respect the rights of Holy Mother Church or hold to the Church's teaching and Her teaching authority. He not only had a very lofty idea of our duties and our obligations to Holy Mother Church. He also had the common touch, with a heart full of love for the people and popular piety. The Cardinal was made a sub-deacon in Prague in September 1887 where he clearly

8 Alejandro Dieguez, *L'Archivio Particolare di Pio X* (Vatican City: Archivio Segreto Vaticano, 2003).
9 Lawrence F. Barman, *Baron Friedrich von Hügel and the Modernist Crisis in England* (Cambridge: Cambridge University Press, 1972), p. 248.

acquired a devotion to the Infant Jesus of Prague, the miracle worker, who promises us that the more we love him, the more he can do for us. Later on in life, the Cardinal was instrumental in promoting awareness of the largest shrine to the Infant of Prague outside Prague, in Arenzano near Genoa. On 7 September 1924 he crowned the statue in his capacity as Archpriest of St Peter's, a great honour for the crowds at Arenzano who received him enthusiastically. He mentioned what a personal significance the honour had for him, given that he had begun his ministry in the Church in Prague. He also made four trips to Riese, birthplace of Pope St Pius X, which is a modest backwater, but he loved it for that reason and because it reminded him of the evangelical counsel of poverty which he himself practised and which the Pope had known all his life. His attraction to Arabba in the Dolomites, where he spent some of his summers in the later years of his life, bears out his aversion to luxury, and love of the simple life, and purity. He commented on the simplicity, poverty and, above all, the piety of the peasants in the mountains, who worked and prayed so hard. The main church in Arabba is dedicated to Our Lady of Mount Carmel and to this day records the memory of the great man who used to stay there. Finally, he was drawn to the Franciscan shrines around Rieti where, likewise, he enjoyed the simplicity, peace and lack of adornment when he was permitted to withdraw from his Roman obligations.

Cardinal Merry del Val also spoke in public at conferences organized by the international league of Catholic women in Rome in 1922, 1925 and 1930. His speeches there appear in this volume, translated into English from the Italian for the first time. These are unapologetically in favour of women resisting all the ploys to 'modernize' and adapt to the spirit of the times. The addresses demonstrate with what vigour he was prepared to come to the assistance of at least half of the world's population. The Cardinal sensed that Feminism was yet one more of the deceptive disguises of the Modernist heresy. His voice becomes prophetic in a truly biblical sense in the last of these three discourses, which was read out after his death. In no uncertain terms, the Cardinal warns women against mixed marriages, frivolity and the rising tide of neo-paganism. What is at stake, he argues, is the Christian ideal of self-sacrifice and renunciation, undermined at every turn by immorality. In other letters he states that there is a war to end all wars going on between Almighty God and Satan for the control of the world. On 6 May 1915 there is a general lament regarding de-christianization: 'a nice mess man makes of the world when he tries to do without God', he says. The last posthumous address warns women not to participate as useful tools in the universal capitulation to evil. On 4 November 1921, he tells Cardinal William Henry O'Connell of Boston that he is not happy about the direction of the Church Militant in this battle, saying famously, of the Church under the new pontiff, 'we are drifting'. He expands: 'How far we may drift I dread to think and how hard it will be later on to get back to our only safe tracks, if we are to regain what we have lost . . .' What would he have thought of Cardinal Siri, over forty years after this pronouncement, who famously said of the pontificate of Pope John XXIII that it would take the Church forty years to recover from his four years at the helm?

However, Cardinal Merry del Val never yielded to despair. There is a cheerful confidence that the good can still find their way. In a letter dated 30 September 1907 to the Cardinal Archbishop of Boston he says of a friend: 'He is really good and I cannot speak too highly of him in every way. He deserves a good wife and any girl may consider herself favoured to have such a husband. I sincerely hope that God will bless his prospects.' The determination to come to the defence of women may be in part due to his love and devotion to his own parents. The letters he wrote to them from school in England are a jewel. His Spanish grandfather was a Carlist, of which little Rafael, aged nine, disapproved. He explains that the Pope is not a Carlist, and thus ends his letter with a warning: 'Do not insult the clergy'. In another letter he says to his mother: 'I am at the top of my class where I hope to remain', with no trace of the humility for which he later became famous. But we can excuse him this pomposity at the age of ten. He signs off with all the respect, dignity and formality of a kind more typical in the nineteenth century '. . . with love to you Papa and all I remain your affectionate son Rafael Merry del Val'. At the age of twenty-six he wrote to his mother from Venice on 31 October 1891 saying: 'I hope you are doing well and are as brave as I should wish. I want to be proud

of you in that respect as I am in others . . .' The young priest begs
for prayers for his cause, the conversion of England, and for his
daily struggles. His mother will obtain all she asks for '. . . if you
kneel on the mountaintop of your virtues and hold up your arms
in prayer for me, while I am fighting the enemy below . . .' In the
notes he writes to himself on one of his many Ignatian retreats,
he reminds himself that he had the grace of a good home and
good parents, that he had not been placed by God 'amongst idol-
aters, Protestants, Schismatics and dangerous or evil company'.
He has no excuse not to become a saint. Or, as he put it to his
nephew Rafaelito in a letter dated 12 February 1907: 'God bless
you, my dear boy, and make you a saint, for his glory and your
own happiness.' The desire to protect the young and guide them
on their way we have already seen in his apostolic labours in
Trastevere. Indeed, he always had a special devotion to the
young saint of holy purity, the Jesuit, St Stanislaus Kostka. The
Rector of the Jesuit school that educated him briefly in Namur,
in Belgium, when his parents were living in Brussels at the
Spanish Embassy, in fact gave him a relic of St Stanislaus.[10] On
his peace mission to Canada in 1897 he was known as another St
Aloysius Gonzaga for the same reason. In Rome he was known
as the 'angel of the Vatican'.

Many of the testimonials for his cause also state that the Cardinal practised penance to a heroic degree, and the nuns and
Monsignor Canali, his private secretary, all state that there were
bloodstains on the walls of his apartment from all the penitential
instruments he had used. The picture emerges of a great priest –
modelled after the greatest priest of all, our Lord, Jesus Christ –
whose belief in purity of the body, heart, soul and mind, was
matched by his devotion to the purity of the Church's doctrines
and dogmas. His confessor, Fr Celestino Alisiardi, stated that he
went to confession once a week all the time he was in Rome, and
that he was punctilious about reading his breviary, making a
daily meditation and examination of conscience. That holy families produce holy vocations was not lost on him. As protector of
the Holy House of Loreto in Italy it seems, thus, all of a piece,

[10] Letter from Cardinal Merry del Val to Albert Latour in Namur, dated
27 November 1928.

that he should have leapt to the defence of the house carried by the angels from Nazareth to the coast of Italy, to protect it from attacks by the Infidel, and installed there intact, miraculously resting there without any support. The Modernists were particularly cynical and skeptical about miracles. He was disappointed with Fr Thurston, SJ, for an article he published in *The Month* in 1912, contributing to the attack on the tradition of recognizing the translation of the Holy House of Nazareth to Loreto as a miracle. Cardinal Merry del Val had written on 28 March 1911 to a priest called Fr George Phillips of the necessity of defending the authenticity of the Holy House. There is a 'venerable tradition with arguments which cannot be swept aside with supercilious and often negative criticism to the detriment of so much that is dear to every Catholic heart'.

Cardinal Merry del Val's deepest love was for Our Lady of Sorrows. He commissioned a portrait of her that is still kept in the Spanish College, which depicts her in an unusual pose. Cardinal Merry del Val departed from the conventions of the genre, since our Lady is normally shown with seven swords piercing her heart, or with one sword to symbolize the seven. He asked the artist for a modification. Our Lady is totally and unambiguously desolate. She neither holds her divine Son in her arms, as Michelangelo depicts her in St Peter's, nor is she crying uncontrollably, as is sometimes the case in more baroque representations. She has no swords penetrating her Immaculate Heart. Her hands rest on a table in what looks like a humble kitchen in a humble dwelling, which is why she is not idealized, but dressed in stylized nineteenth-century peasant attire. Her hands are clasped, but not dramatically. It is as if they are too heavy for her to control, such is the extreme weakness of her body, heart and soul, at the death of her divine Son. Our Lady neither looks down at her hands, nor out of the window. She is not crying. She simply looks absolutely desolate and bereft, as if she has been utterly abandoned. The Servites have a special devotion to Our Lady of Sorrows, and the Cardinal became a member of the Third Order in 1900, which indicates that he spent at least thirty years of his life particularly devoted to Our Lady of Sorrows. Monsignor Canali relates that he said the rosary every day as well as the chaplet of the Seven Sorrows of

Our Lady. Indeed, he slept with a rosary in his hand.

One of the most eloquent of the Cardinal's recollections concerns our Lady and her sorrows, and we are very pleased to be able to publish it here for the first time. This will interest those who already understand the link between Our Lady of Sorrows and her last two titles, yet to be defined *ex cathedra*. The Church has always believed that our Lady is the Co-Redemptrix and Mediatrix of all Graces. Her appearance at Fatima in 1917 outlined all that she can do for us if we remain true to the rosary and the brown scapular, stop offending God, and practise the communions and confessions of reparation for the five sins against the Immaculate Heart of Mary which are bringing down the wrath of God upon us. She asks the pope, in union with the bishops of the whole world, to consecrate Russia to her Immaculate Heart, points to God's mercy, happy as He will be to write off the debt humanity has incurred by embracing the deviant form of atheism with which Russian Communism has been associated from 1917 onwards. The Cardinal points out the links between Our Lady of Sorrows and her two roles of mediating all the graces Christ won for us on Calvary, to perfection, demonstrating that God bestowed upon our Lady at Calvary her ability to be the greatest channel of graces into the world after the Redeemer. Her sorrows at the foot of the Cross really were without parallel. God will refuse her nothing. The Church's progress through history and time is slow, and we all still await the day when the consecration is made and our Lady given the due she deserves, ushering in the longed-for era of peace also promised at Fatima once humanity has expiated its debt through prayers, penance and sacrifices of the kind outlined at Fatima.

With the exception of three public discourses on the dangers posed by neo-paganism to modern women, our selection of the Cardinal's spiritual writings lays no particular stress on the Cardinal's role as defender of the Faith in the Church Militant. Rather it focuses on his labours as a shepherd of souls, since this is what he asked to have inscribed on his tomb in the crypt of St Peter's: 'Souls, souls, give me souls, take all else away'. There are some of the published letters of direction he wrote to some of his penitents, converts and spiritual children. All of the instructions and guidance demonstrate that he was a simple, practical, direct and effective shepherd and guardian of souls. We also include some of his recollections given on retreats, and in full all of the indulgenced prayers he wrote, now contained in the *Raccolta* of the Church. Some of the letters of direction were last made available in America in 1964 as *The Spiritual Diary of Raphael Cardinal Merry del Val* and in England in 1974 by the Legion of Merry del Val with the title *Let God Act*, edited by Sister Paula Fairlie, OSB, with an introduction by Bishop Peter Canisius van Lierde, Vicar General of His Holiness for Vatican City. They were reprinted again by the Carmelite Monastery at Quidenham in Norfolk in 1977, 1979 and 1986. Our text is, in fact, a faithful copy of this edition, reprinted with the kind permission of the nuns, but extended on account of the new translations and texts, which help to fill in the picture of the Cardinal as a shepherd of souls. For the last twenty years these editions have all been out of print in English.

The letters form a comprehensive guide to the spiritual life suitable for lay Catholics who take seriously the call to personal holiness. The writings reflect the Cardinal's great sense of humility, his Franciscan spirituality and love of poverty, his war on human respect as detrimental to holiness and truth, his devotion to the Sacred Heart, his love of self-sacrifice, his devotion to the sacraments, and his overwhelming sense of the power of God's love and God's will, which gave us the simple dictum and injunction to abandon everything for God, 'Let God act!' That abandonment to the Will of God links him to Fr Jean-Pierre de Caussade, SJ and the Carmelite Brother Laurence of the Resurrection, whose classic expositions of complete trust in Divine Providence echo throughout. Cardinal Merry del Val's more pithy reflections are also aimed at destroying the kinds of pettiness and scruples that prevent spiritual health and progress. He has none of the literary style of St Francis de Sales, since there is no imagery; there are virtually no references to the Church Doctors and Church Fathers.[11] His writing therefore does not burden the imagination, intellect and conscience. Rather, with a few, sparing references to Holy Scripture the Cardinal attempts

---

[11] See St Francis de Sales, *Mystical Flora*, translated by C. Mulholland (Leominster: Gracewing, 2002).

to inspire confidence in hearts and souls. Perseverance is what he believed was crucial. The Church is there to support those who can, will and do persevere in the spiritual life, in spite of all the trials, temptations and sorrows that our Lord promised us. It is a great sadness that the full and complete story of the Cardinal may never be known. The correspondence with Fr Denis Sheil has mysteriously disappeared, although the Birmingham Oratory is still trying to track it down. It is said that there was a mysterious fire in the study of Monsignor Canali who, as the Cardinal's private secretary for thirty years, was instrumental in collecting all the papers for the cause after 1953 and who was in fact the source behind Pio Cenci's original biography, having worked daily with the Cardinal, and knew his way round his papers. The fire must have destroyed many of his and the Cardinal's papers. Those who wish to consult all the sources concerning the entire life of the Cardinal are meanwhile directed to the compilation by Pio Cenci, who worked at the Secret Vatican Archives and was the first to produce a serious study of the documents in 1933, three years after the Cardinal's premature death from appendicitis. It has an introduction by Pope Pius XII, then Cardinal Pacelli, who had been something of a protégé of the Cardinal.[12] A more accessible biography for the general public by Marie Cecilia Buehrle has recently been reissued.[13] Those who love the Cardinal are kindly asked to report favours received to the Spanish College, Rome.[14]

---

[12] Pio Cenci, *Il Cardinale Raffaele Merry del Val* (Torino: Lice, 1933, reprinted Rome: Tip. Poliglotta Vaticana, 1955).

[13] Marie Cecilia Buehrle, *Rafael Cardinal Merry del Val* (London: Sands & Co., 1957), available from Carmel Books.

[14] Thanks to Most Rev. Fr Sergio Pagano, Prefect of the Secret Vatican Archives, for his kind invitation to consult the Vatican's holdings. Thanks also to Miss Madeleine Beard, and Sr Mary Joseph, OSB, of the Venerable English College (Rome), for editorial assistance, and to the archivists of the archdioceses of Westminster and Southwark, especially Frs Ian Dickie and Michael Clifton. Special thanks also to the staff of the archdiocesan archives of Paris and Boston; to Rev. Thomas McCoog, SJ, of the Jesuit Archives, Farm Street; to the staff of the libraries at the University of St Andrews, the University of Durham and the University of Georgetown (Washington, DC); but chiefly to Mgr Tomás-Amable Díez Olano of the Spanish College (Rome) and Alejandro Dieguez, MA, of the Secret Vatican Archives for their patience and kindness.

Important dates in the life of Cardinal Merry Del Val

1865   10 October, birth in London
1875   First Holy Communion
        Schooling at Remington's, Bournemouth
1876   Attends the College of Our Lady of Peace, Namur, Belgium
1878   Attendance at Jesuit College of St Michael, Brussels
1883   Enters the seminary of St Cuthbert's, Ushaw, County Durham
1885   Scots College Rome, where he receives minor orders
        Pope Leo XIII sends him to the Accademia dei Nobili Ecclesiastici
        in Rome
1887   September, Prague, where he is ordained subdeacon at the hands of
        Cardinal Schönborn, Prince Archbishop of Prague in the Cathedral
        of St Vitus
        Private Chamberlain to the Pope with the title of Monsignor; sent
        to London as secretary to Monsignor Ruffo Scilla to offer
        congratulations to Queen Victoria on her Golden Jubilee
1888   Named secretary to the Special Papal Mission to Berlin for the
        funeral of Emperor William I and the coronation of Emperor
        Frederick III
        30 December, ordained by Cardinal Parrocchi, Vicar of Rome
1889   1 January says First Mass at the shrine of St Ignatius in the Gesù
        in Rome
1889   Easter, Scots College villa near Marino in the Alban Hills
        Named secretary of the Special Papal Mission to the Imperial Court
        of Vienna
1890   Helps materially in the founding of the Spanish College in Rome
1891   Appointed a Papal Chamberlain on active duty with His Holiness
1892   Earns doctorate of Theology and degree in Canon Law from
        Accademia
1893   Named Apostolic Delegate to Hungary to present the Red Hat to
        the new Cardinal Lawrence Schlauch, Bishop of Gran Varadino
1895   Named Associate Secretary of the Special Papal Commission for
        the Union of Dissident Churches
1896   Named Secretary of the Special Commission of Cardinals for the
        study of the validity of Anglican Orders
1897   Appointed Domestic Prelate by His Holiness and Special Apostolic
        Delegate to Canada
1898   Named a Consultor of the Sacred Congregation of the Index
1899   Chosen President of the Pontificia Accademia dei Nobili
        Ecclesiastici; beginning of his friendship with Nicola Canali, later
        his private secretary and then a Cardinal
1900   19 April, named titular Archbishop of Nicaea

6 May, consecrated same by Cardinal Rampolla in the church of Our Lady of Montserrat, Rome; becomes a member of the Third Order of the Servites

1902 Sent as Special Envoy to London for the Coronation of King Edward VII

1903 Made Secretary of the Sacred College and Secretary of the Conclave in the election of Pope St Pius X

Appointed Pro-Secretary of State

Appointed Secretary of State and a Cardinal of the Holy Roman Church by Pope St Pius X; Cardinal Priest of Santa Prassede, Rome; beginning of Fr Alisiardi, SJ's spiritual direction

1905 Separation of Church and State in France

1907 Publication of *Pascendi*, the encyclical against Modernism

1909 Publication of *The Truth of Papal Claims*, apologetic work by Merry del Val

1914 After sudden death of Cardinal Rampolla, nominated Archpriest of St Peter's

Appointed Secretary of the Sacred Congregation of the Holy Office; Concordat with Serbia; death of Pope St Pius X on 20 August

1920 Sent as Papal Legate to Assisi for the first centenary of the finding of the body of St Francis of Assisi

1922 Pope Benedict XV asks the Cardinal to preside over a congress of the International Women's League

1924 7 September, travels to the Sanctuary of Arenzano, near Genoa, for the Coronation of the Infant Jesus of Prague

1925 Cardinal addresses the International Women's League again

Celebrates his Silver Jubilee as priest

1926 Sent as Papal Legate to Assisi for the seventh centenary of the death of St Francis of Assisi

1927 22 August, Feast of the Immaculate Heart of Mary, returns to Ushaw

25 August, plants tree there

1928 Celebrates his Silver Jubilee as a Cardinal

1929 6 May, appointed Cardinal Protector of the Venerable English College, Rome, for a nine-month period

December, Beatification of the Martyrs of England and Wales, of whom forty were canonized in 1970

1930 26 February, his holy death in Vatican City

Spiritual Writings

Prayers

Morning offering for a pure intention

I have promised with God's grace:
  Not to begin any action without remembering that *He is
  witness* of it;
  That He *performs* it together with me and *gives me the
  means* to do it;
  Never to conclude any without the same thought, offering
  it to Him as belonging to Him;
  And in the course of the action, whenever the same thought
  shall occur, to stop for a moment and renew the desire of
  pleasing Him.

Litany of humility
*(said every day after Holy Mass, and composed on
24 February 1895)*

O Jesus! Meek and humble of heart, Hear me.
From the desire of being esteemed, Deliver me Jesus.
From the desire of being loved, Deliver me Jesus.
From the desire of being extolled, Deliver me Jesus.
From the desire of being honoured, Deliver me Jesus.
From the desire of being praised, Deliver me Jesus.
From the desire of being preferred to others, Deliver me Jesus.
From the desire of being consulted, Deliver me Jesus.
From the desire of being approved, Deliver me Jesus.
From the fear of being humiliated, Deliver me Jesus.
From the fear of being despised, Deliver me Jesus.

From the fear of suffering rebukes, Deliver me Jesus.
From the fear of being calumniated, Deliver me Jesus.
From the fear of being forgotten, Deliver me Jesus.
From the fear of being ridiculed, Deliver me Jesus.
From the fear of being wronged, Deliver me Jesus.
From the fear of being suspected, Deliver me Jesus.

That others may be loved more than I, Jesus, grant me the
grace to desire it.
That others may be esteemed more than I, Jesus, grant me the
grace to desire it.
That in the opinion of the world, others may increase, and that
I may decrease, Jesus, grant me the grace to desire it.
That others may be chosen and I set aside, Jesus, grant me the
grace to desire it.
That others may be praised and I unnoticed, Jesus, grant me
the grace to desire it.
That others may be preferred to me in everything, Jesus, grant
me the grace to desire it.
That others may become holier than I, provided that I become
as holy as I should, Jesus, grant me the grace to desire it.

Indulgenced prayers by the Servant of God in the *Raccolta*

My dearest Jesus, teach me to be patient, when all the day
long my heart is troubled by little, but vexatious crosses.
(*Indulgence of 300 days*)

O dearly beloved Word of God, teach me to be generous, to
serve Thee as Thou dost deserve, to give without counting the
cost, to fight without fretting at my wounds, to labour without
seeking repose, to be prodigal of myself without looking for
any other reward save that of knowing that I do Thy holy will.
(*Indulgence of 500 days*)

Change my heart, O Jesus, Thou who didst empty Thyself for
love of me! Make known to my spirit how excellent were Thy

sacred humiliations. Let me begin this day, illumined by Thy divine light, to do away with that portion of the natural man that still lives undiminished in me. This is the chief source of my misery, this the barrier that I constantly oppose to Thy love. (*Indulgence of 500 days*)

O merciful Lord, Thou art never weary of speaking to my poor heart; grant me the grace that, if today I hear Thy voice, my heart may not be hardened. (*Indulgence of 300 days*)

Lord, I am nothing, but although nothing, I adore thee. (*Indulgence of 300 days*)

Lord, I am my own enemy, when I seek my peace apart from Thee. (*Indulgence of 300 days*)

O my soul, love the Love that loves thee from eternity. (*Indulgence of 300 days*)

At thy feet, O my Jesus, I prostrate myself and I offer Thee the repentance of my contrite heart, which is humbled in its nothingness and in Thy holy presence. I adore Thee in the Sacrament of Thy love, the ineffable Eucharist. I desire to receive Thee into the poor dwelling that my heart offers Thee. While waiting for the happiness of sacramental Communion, I wish to possess Thee in spirit. Come to me, O my Jesus, since I, for my part, am coming to Thee! May Thy love embrace my whole being in life and in death. I believe in Thee, I hope in Thee, I love Thee.

To the Sacred Heart
(*written 1889–1890*)

I

Jesus, Thy Heart has loved me well
For more than I love Thee
I seek in vain, I cannot tell
Why Thou should'st so love me

II

T'was not my wealth that made Thee turn
From Heaven's bright home alone
And caused Thy Sacred Heart to burn
With that sweet flame of love

III

What is there I can call my own
That was not ever Thine?
On earth my All, in Heaven my crown
Yes, nought but sin is mine

IV

Nor was it that Thou had'st foretold
That I would grateful be
Thou knowest that my heart grown cold
Would not remember Thee

V

O Jesus, tell me then I pray
What I have sought in vain
The Midnight Cave, and Calvary, say
Why so much love and pain?

VI

Child, I saw thee in Satan's hands
Suffering and in woe
My Heart so longed to break those bands
My love to crush the foe

VII

I saw that dear ungrateful man
Would leave the path of life
But then, henceforth through Me he can
Be victor in the strife

VIII

I wished poor souls to understand
That I had done my part
And by the Cross, to take their stand
With hopeful loving heart

IX

O Sacred love, My Lord, My all,
A God could love like this
And almost make that first man's fall
A constant source of bliss

X

Henceforth Sweet Lord the World's renown
With me shall have no part
Like Thee, I'll seek a thorny crown
And love Thy Sacred Heart.

The Secret of the Saints
(*1898*)

To play through life a perfect part
Unnoticed and unknown
To seek no rest in any heart
Save only God's alone;
In little things to own no will
To have no share in great
To find the labour ready still
And for the crown to wait.

Upon the brow to bear no trace
Of more than common care
To write no secret in the face
For men to read it there
The daily cross to clasp and bless
With such familiar zeal
As hides from all that not the less
The daily weight you feel.

In trials that praise will never pay
To see your life go past
To meet in every evening day
Twin sister of the last;
To hear of high heroic things
And yield them severance due
But feel life's daily offerings
Are far more fit for you.

To woo no secret soft disguise
To which self-love is prone
Unnoticed by all other eyes
Unworthy in your own;
To yield with such a happy art
That no one thinks you care
And say to your poor bleeding heart
'How little can you bear'.

Note to Himself after An Ignatian Retreat

Beautiful Mother, why have I not loved thee as I ought. Oh my Jesus do please teach me how to hate from the very bottom of my heart all applause, esteem of men, and to work only for thee in thy sight, hidden away in the depths of a really interior life . . . My God why am I not in Hell? Where is Thy Justice? Oh mystery. Thou hast spared me and condemned so many. Oh how I hate myself: not so much out of fear of Thy Justice but because I have trampled on Thy love and on Thy mercy. Mary, take me by the hand and lead me to Calvary. I want no other home.

Prayer for the Conversion of England
(*1895*)

O Blessed Virgin Mary, Mother of God and our most gentle Queen and Mother, look down in mercy upon England thy Dowry and upon us all who greatly hope and trust in thee. By thee it was that Jesus our Saviour and our hope was given unto the world; and He has given thee to us that we might hope still more. Plead for us thy children, whom thou didst receive and accept at the foot of the Cross, O sorrowful Mother! Intercede for our separated brethren, that with us in the one true fold they may be united to the supreme Shepherd, the Vicar of thy Son. Pray for us all, dear Mother, that by faith fruitful in good works we may all deserve to see and praise God, together with thee, in our heavenly home. Amen.

Rule of Life

When he first began to direct me the Cardinal said to me:
Draw up a rule of life, and be as faithful to it as a nun is to her Rule.

You know the line of conduct marked out for you; you know the way by which you ought to walk. Follow it, and you will find Jesus.

Do not lightly make promises which you cannot keep. The devil insinuates himself into these things and uses them to make us lose our peace of mind. Whatever comes from him disturbs us and takes away our peace.

When we have made promises to God which we know are according to His will, and thus pleasing to Him, we must remain faithful to them, without wavering, even if an angel were to advise us to do otherwise.

As far as possible, have a fixed time for your spiritual exercises, and do not change the time for a mere whim. Nevertheless, accept patiently any circumstances independent of your will which upset your arrangements. Then put them off until later.

Every rule I give you must give way to the demands of your family life, whether these be foreseen or unforeseen. You will have to adapt your spiritual exercises a little according to the circumstances in which you find yourself. Of necessity your kind of life cannot be very uniform: what really matters is that the essentials should remain unchanged.

Remember that the circumstances which you yourself have not occasioned, are God's messengers. They come a thousand times a day to tell you the different ways in which you may show Him your love. I am sure you would not feel upset if your Guardian Angel spoke and said to you now and then:

'Come here. Do that', and again 'Change everything: that is no longer what the Master requires of you, He wants something else'.

Well then, heed this voice in the happenings of every hour when they do not depend on you and you are not free to alter them. When, on the other hand, you can control them, then make haste to resume your ordinary way of life. Take up what has been laid down for you, without a moment's delay, and let all resume its usual order. But when everything is unexpectedly turned upside down against your will, then have what I should call 'a great elasticity' and, without showing your feelings, go and deal with the situation and take God with you. If, instead of praying or performing an act of piety, you are required to do something else which you would rather not do, do it for God. Ask Him to sanctify that which is not in itself holy, and be at peace, for you will be showing yourself His faithful servant.

You must understand, and accept as a fixed principle, that every indisposition or illness is a clear indication of the will of God. It is better than any direction for as long as it lasts it indicates the precise manner in which you ought to serve and love Him. When you are sick every obligation, promise or accepted practice remains suspended. You must not then consider yourself obliged to do anything. The good God is taking it upon Himself to show you the work He deigns to accept from you. This readiness to change your usual way of doing things as the divine will reveals itself, is an act of solid virtue, and proof that you prefer God's will to your own.

You tell me that you feel as though you were rowing against the current. But is this not a sign that you are going the right way? If you were aware of no resistance, and went with the stream, then there would be good reason to fear.

Virtue is always against the current. You say you would not much mind the effort if you thought any good purpose were served. But not merely may you hope that it is; you may be sure of it. The very effort is already a success, provided that it is generous and persevering. Real success is not your affair. Leave that to God. He will forget nothing ... For the moment your reward must be to know that you are doing His will.

Yes, during your absence, I see no reason why you should not go less frequently to confession whilst still continuing your communions. You would do well to give a little time to working for the poor, especially when you are with others. This will be a sustaining force and help you to avert many small faults.

Let us never act with the intention of pleasing the world. Let us have the courage to bear the world's criticisms and disapproval, and have no false respect of persons. Provided God is pleased, what does the rest matter?

One should not do good with the intention of obtaining the world's esteem, but neither should one refrain from doing good for fear of being noticed. Act with simplicity and detachment, for God alone and under His gaze, without concerning yourself with anything else.

You must not refrain from doing good from fear of the thought of vainglory which may arise. This is a temptation which must be resisted. At the beginning of your actions offer them to our Lord and you will thus safeguard yourself against finishing for Satan an action begun for Jesus.

You need not make it a rule always to choose what is most repugnant to you. Whether we like a thing or not is of no importance in itself. What really matters is knowing where the will of God lies, His glory, our duty, and to decide on those grounds.

Submission to the Will of God

You have understood me perfectly in making only a simple promise, but try to gain strength to put yourself *absolutely* into the hands of God, and to desire before all that His will be done whatever be the sacrifice He may ask of you. 'To will all that God does: to do all that God wills'. That is what can draw you nearer the Heart of our Lord, and that should be your motto in great things and in small. Be grateful to Him and shown Him boundless confidence. Think how He loves you with a tenderness you will never be able to fathom ... Pray without ceasing for He wills His graces to reach us through the medium of our poverty. But when we have prayed, and prayed much, let us leave our hopes, our fears and our troubles in His hands. He knows better than we what is good for us, and we should sit at His feet and rejoice if He deigns to show us that we have been mistaken. He can make those efforts and prayers of our weakness serve for something better still! Therefore take heart!

'What is the use of praying?' In order to give God what He asks of us in His love, and to make it the foundation of His benefits and of an everlasting crown. Nor let us forget that prayer is not only a duty but a necessity, an act of virtue, and that, whether or not it be heard in the way we wish, it remains, and will always remain, an act of virtue which will one day be the source of our happiness.

Life here below is not the true life. Death is not the end of life but the gate which opens into life eternal. The love of God wills for us the life which is happiness in Him. He wills to save us from hell which is the real death.

See our Lord in every happening of your life. See everything as ordered by His will, His loving-kindness, and then you will always be at peace.

Do your best and leave the rest to God. He does not ask your success, but your good will.

Let God act. Do not forestall events and do not dwell upon and worry yourself over what may happen to you. Leave all that to God. You have only to submit and obey.

However, we must not expect the will of God to be made known to us in everything by some heavenly intervention. At times it is shown to us by the most ordinary, everyday circumstances. Then we must recognize it, see it in the events which He permits, which are beyond our control, and be docile in thus following the divine will in everything.

We must serve God from love and not from fear. When our Lord appeared to His Apostles He gave them peace, and when He departed from them it was still peace which He left them.

The love of God ought to be in our will, not only in our feelings. The feelings which our heart experiences depend upon our will. What really matters is to prefer God to all else: to be ready to sacrifice all rather than consent to sin. Our will should always be in that disposition.

Our will is like a rock in the sea. The waves may wash around and even submerge it, but there it remains immovable; and when the sea dies down after the storm, it leaves it intact. So our will may remain firm despite all our feelings.

When we have to make a decision, and it is impossible to ask advice, let us first pray, ask God for light, reflect, wait, steady ourselves, think what we should wish to have done at the moment of our death, and only then decide.

You ought to live in abiding peace, for our Lord is with you and that is enough. Let Him speak to you and guide you, but do not listen to the tumult of your fears which drown His voice and do not raise this fantastic dust which dims His light!

You must allow God to act and not want to do too much by yourself, for then you cannot feel the effect of the grace He is giving you. This is quite as important, perhaps even more important, than the efforts you make to overcome yourself in the particular difficulty of the present moment.

Do not be surprised that you are aware of opposition within yourself. It is the struggle between nature and grace; it is inevitable, and if there were no effort there would be no merit. Provided that grace triumphs, everything is for the best.

Open the windows! Dilate your heart, act with the liberty of the children of God. Your conscience must be big and wide, not narrow and cramped. Have boundless trust in the Heart of Jesus.

You must have a delicate conscience, but beware of scruples. A scruple consists in seeing sin where there is none. Obedience is the only safeguard.

You must be detached from all that is not God. You must accept His good pleasure in everything, without worrying yourself and without seeking satisfaction in creatures.

When God asks for sacrifices He does so gently, and inspirations which come from Him cause no disturbance.

Anything which troubles us is not from the Spirit of God. The Holy Spirit gives peace.

Allow yourself to be gently led by grace. Abandon yourself to God's guidance, leaving to Him the daily working out of your life, without making so many efforts to act on your own initiative.

When you are fearful and foresee trials, say at once 'Very well, I accept them'.

The Imitation of Christ

Imbue yourself with the thought of the sufferings of our Lord. Make every effort to detach yourself from what is transitory; from vanities and from things of this world, for all that passes away so quickly. Place your hope, your thoughts and your heart in those things which are above and which are eternal.

Honour and wonder at the weakness of the Child Jesus, who willed to be little and weak for love of us. Accept your weakness and rest in our Lady's arms, rejoicing that you are unable to do what you would like. Our Lord also was weak, and He glorified His Father by His powerlessness and His weakness in the manger. He also glorified Him on the Cross. So, in union with Him, you should accept the sacrifices which your state of health imposes on you. You must be docile as a child, remembering that He has said that those who are not as little children will not enter into the kingdom of heaven.

Jesus loved poverty and obedience; therefore try to love these virtues and practise them. He was humble, forgotten, misunderstood; for love of Him consent peacefully to be humiliated, to be overlooked. These are the things which God allows so that we may be brought closer to Him; they are the steps we have to climb in order to reach Him.

Consider how the Holy Family was founded on humility. It is by humility in your relations with your family that you will attain peace. Our Lord spent thirty years of His life in teaching us the humble domestic virtues, to make us understand their importance and to merit for us the grace to imitate Him.

Practise humility, not by seeking out occasions, but by accepting those which present themselves. Offer them to our Lord. Let your opinion give way to others when duty does not forbid it. Accept the difficulties and the aridity in your religious exercises, humbly recognizing that you are nothing, but without being discouraged.

The first and most important lesson which our Lord gives

us is *humility*, humility of mind, of will, of heart. We must try to imitate the humility of the Heart of Jesus, His union with the Father, His self-abandonment, His conformity to the will of His Father. Strive to be like Him, utterly given over to the will of God; in little things as well as great, in everyday trials, and in the difficulties of life.

Everything must serve to hasten the progress of our spiritual life. We have no time to lose. We must profit by every day, every moment, every circumstance, in order to become better and more united to God. Ask our Lady to obtain you this grace.

We must always give God the first place, and our duty to Him must come before everything else. You must never hesitate when your duty to Him is in question. Do not omit to do something because it may displease others and cause you to be criticized. Rather, fulfil your duty bravely and without weakness. Remember to meditate on those words of Jesus: 'The Lord thy God shalt thou adore and Him only shalt thou serve'.

The name of Jesus should be your hope and refuge in temptation, your help against the devil. Do not doubt Him, but love Him for the infinite love He bears you. This name is the expression of all our Lord is for you, of all that you must be for Him.

Let us practise the presence of God by making a sanctuary of our heart where we can find Him, that He may be the companion of our life.

Try to love without seeing. Often one loves because one sees but we must also love without seeing.

The touchstone whereby to recognize a good spirit and good inspirations is *obedience*. When we try to withdraw ourselves from the submission and obedience we owe to the Church and our superiors it is obvious that we are not led by a good spirit. We can never be mistaken in obeying.

God created us *for Himself*. We cannot escape Him. If we refuse to go to Him by love we shall fall at the feet of His justice.

God allows secondary causes to act. By these words we mean to say that He permits us to act according to our free will, that He rarely intervenes with miracles, permitting the natural laws ordered by Him to operate. But that does not alter the fact that we must believe that *everything* comes from His Providence and that He watches over us unceasingly and orders everything, at every instant, for our good.

Try to copy the humility of the Heart of Jesus as shown in the lowliness of His Eucharistic life, His abnegation, His forgetfulness of self. As He 'emptied' Himself before His Father for love of us, so should we likewise strive to forget ourselves for love of Him.

Have a great devotion to the Passion of our Lord. Think of the love He showed us when He allowed His Heart to be pierced to prove that love to us. Prove yours to Him by accepting sufferings and trials for His love. Let pain open your heart as it opened His.

The Spirit of Faith

Superstition is contrary to faith. You must banish all superstitious fears for it is unthinkable that God should make important events depend upon something which is futile and ambiguous.

Faith is the gift of God. We must ask it in prayer, and thank Him for this grace, which is not given to all. When we have the happiness of the Faith, we should be filled with compassion for those who do not have the same light. We must be patient with them and sympathize with their situation. In our own faith we must submit our intelligence, for if everything were always evident as it is in Heaven, we would have no merit in believing.

It is not possible to sin against faith without an act of the will. We must lay down our will at the foot of the throne of God and pay Him the homage of our belief.

We must be disposed to believe that which escapes the narrow limits of our intelligence. Recognize your limitations.

The secret of sanctity is to see God in all things; our faith must be based on love and on confidence in God.

Let us often remind ourselves that there is not a single

instant of the day or a circumstance of our life which is not permitted or willed by God.

Goodness does not consist in sentiments but in interior mortification and in the virtues attained in faithfully performing our duty in order to do the will of God. Make this the basis and foundation of all your efforts.

We can lose the sensible presence of Jesus. We must never then think He is far from us. He is nearer than before, for we are suffering. Do not give up prayer at such times! Let us pray though it be without consolation. Let us be on our guard against comforting ourselves by means of worldly distractions. Let us seek Jesus in prayer; seek Him in church; and there we shall find Him.

You must not dread temptations or, above all, worry yourself over them, for they intensify our love for our Lord, owing to the efforts we make to resist and overcome, by the grace which He never refuses us if we pray to Him for it.

Reflect that grace means responsibility, and that you must correspond to that which you receive and know how to profit from it.

It is only by knowing how to love God that we shall learn to love others and do them good.

When you hear uncharitable talk which you cannot prevent you ought to be silent and bury what you have heard as in a tomb. You must never consent to sin in order not to displease others. Suffer anything rather than that.

You must have the courage to tell the truth and not shrink from a duty. You must be brave enough to face ridicule, for often what is of obligation is ridiculous in the eyes of the world. Do that for love of our Lord and in order to draw nearer to Him.

The moment we find clever people holding an opinion contrary to that of those who are less intelligent, we must not conclude forthwith that the latter are wrong and the former right. Even a child may have the truth within him.

Filial love or fear is not a defect of confidence – the comparison with the child is excellent. When something frightens a child, he runs to his mother and hides in her arms. Fear will draw the child even closer. It is thus that we ought to behave with God.

Prayer

You should always recollect yourself before you begin to pray. Do not be afraid of losing a little time for that. If you have only a little time at your disposal it is better to shorten your prayer by half, but prepare well for it. It is not necessary to say many prayers, but in order to pray, it is necessary to be recollected and settled in the presence of God.

Do your utmost to pray well. Do not forget that prayer is the basis and foundation of all our progress. On it rests our hope of correcting our faults and growing in the love of God.

Before beginning your meditation ask for the grace to make it well. From the subject of your prayer draw a practical resolution for the day, which will enable you to avoid a fault or to act virtuously and remind yourself of it during the course of the day.

God does not consider the number of prayers we say. He can hear us in an instant, even if we have not made a long prayer, like the labourer in the Gospel, who obtained his recompense after having worked but one hour.

Pray as you would have spoken to our Lord had you had the happiness to approach Him during His mortal life.

Always pray trustfully, for if, when you are praying, you are thinking that He is not going to hear you, it is as though you give with one hand and take away with the other what you have given.

The prayer which best suits you is AMEN. Do not seek after any other formula.

Pray our Lord to give you that peace which He came to bring which makes all things easy and will enlarge your heart.

Ask our Lord for two things:

1. To teach you to know Him. Pray that He will show you the treasures of His Sacred Heart, His loving-kindness, His infinite mercy, His mortification, His tenderness. All the rest you may learn is as nothing in comparison with the knowledge and love of your God.

2. Ask Him to teach you to know yourself better, to see

your own poverty more clearly and your nothingness, so that you may correct yourself and remove everything which is displeasing to God from your soul. Ask that you may see wherein you can serve Him better, and more perfectly fulfil His will in you. Ask our Lady to help you to this humble knowledge of yourself.

Beg the Holy Spirit to form in you a heart like the Heart of Jesus, a heart full of courage, of mortification, of love for God and your neighbour; a heart which shrinks from no sacrifice which knows how to conquer self-love, human respect, and a weakness of nature; a heart after God's Heart.

Ask the Holy Spirit to give you the strength necessary to serve our Lord according to His will, perseveringly, tranquilly, without worrying as to whether what you are doing seems to you easy or difficult; simply acting for our Lord alone, in order to please Him, and keeping your eyes ever fixed upon Him.

We are so tiny, so poor and erratic in all our efforts to serve Him, and He is so great, so loving and constant in His dealings with us, that He is constantly full of pity for us in our flounderings. We should fly to Him with childlike confidence, without any fear that He may ever be disgusted with us.

It is for us to reflect as in a mirror the light of Him who is the true light, but the mirror must be clean and pure.

Let your prayer have an element of sacrifice in it. There is no sacrifice without immolation.

Holy Communion

Be devoted to the Blessed Sacrament in order to obtain final perseverance. Before you retire, go to our Lord and tell Him your failings, beg Him to help and pardon you. Our Lord loves us; He thinks of us unceasingly; His gaze follows us every instant of the day.

Our best Communions are not those which give us great consolation, but those in which we approach Him with humility, contrition and trust.

Let us live from one Communion to the next, accepting and offering to God the trials and contradictions which come our way. Then we shall communicate well.

During the day, let us often make spiritual communions to preserve the presence of our Lord within us.

Beware of absenting yourself from Communion owing to discouragement. It is one of the devil's wiles to make us exaggerate our faults in order to hinder us from receiving Holy Communion, from going to our Lord, and thus to deprive us of His help.

Make your Communions, your prayers, your actions, in a spirit of reparation for the offences committed against the Heart of Jesus!

When you receive Holy Communion think how great is the gift which you receive. Our Lord gives Himself to each one of us individually as if only He and we were in the world.

The best preparation for Communion is the faithful fulfilment of our duties, accepting and offering to God the troubles and opposition that come our way, with the intention of making all these acts of ours serve as a preparation for Holy Communion.

If you are obliged to miss a Communion, endeavour to communicate as soon as possible. The soul must live.

Let us live every day with the very life of Christ and ask Him to come to us on the last day of our life, to give Himself to us for the last time in Holy Viaticum, so that, holding us safely in His hands, He may lead us to the heavenly home of happiness and love.

Confession and Penance

Try not to make confessions which are worthless. That happens when people give more time and care to searching out and counting up their sins than to making sure of their sincere sorrow for them and their firm purpose to amend them.

We cannot hope to enter Heaven alone. We must take others there. Let us toil for souls by example, work and prayer. If necessary let us know how to sacrifice our tastes, our time, and our health.

We should understand that the pity and compassion we feel here on earth – when it is right and sincere – is but a reflection and shadow of the infinite compassion and tender mercy of God. So when we see in sinners and the wretched something which excuses them and lessens their responsibility, we may be sure that God sees that infinitely better than we do. And when we can neither see nor understand it, He excuses and forgives as we would never know how to.

Never despair of the salvation of a soul. This is the teaching of the Church, which never pronounces a sentence of damnation upon anyone; for one instant suffices to lead a soul to God.

Once when I told the Cardinal of my fears for a relative who had died without the sacraments, and my grief, he answered: 'Do you think you love that soul as much as our Lord loves it?'

Our life must be a kind of constant death. For in the measure in which we die to the things of this world, to interior and exterior obstacles, in that degree may we be said to live, for we begin to possess something of the perfect life in eternity – God.

The Spirit of Sacrifice

Cultivate the habit of sacrifice; those little sacrifices which pass unobserved but which God sees: a word, an act of kindness, the sacrifice of little acts of vanity.

Our sins are what made Jesus suffer. Every one of our sins added to His sufferings and was one more thorn in His crown, one more blow at His scourging. There is no question of time, of present or past; for God there is no time. What a consolation for us to think that if, by our efforts, we succeed in corresponding to grace and avoiding sin we shall have spared Jesus and given Him some relief ...

By His sufferings Jesus wished to teach us the value of suffering. By His pain He has merited for us patience in our trials. By His Blood He has won for us all grace. Even one grace is the fruit of His precious Blood. The sacraments are the fruit of His Blood. Let us love, or at least accept, sufferings for love of Him who sends them to us in love. The trials He send us are treasures wherewith to purchase Heaven.

We ought to make the sacrifices asked by our Lord joyfully; peacefully and joyfully. We must not drag our cross but carry it joyously after Jesus.

Do not forget that unless you crucify yourself you will crucify Jesus!

The trials, the contradictions and the sufferings of every day must tighten the bonds which unite you to Him. For by bearing them lovingly, by offering them to Him, you will change them all into everlasting joys, and they will procure you the grace of being more closely united to Him through all eternity.

Our Lord was not content to give us only part of Himself. Learn to be generous with Him and not to measure your sacrifices or be satisfied with merely doing what is necessary to save your soul. Generously give Him what He is asking of you.

Bear your everyday troubles and anxieties peacefully and with resignation. Remember that you cannot be the disciple of Jesus unless you share in His Passion.

Upon this cross, which our Lord is offering you today, offer also your own sacrifice, and be assured that it will bring you still nearer to His divine Heart.

Accept the humiliations and sufferings which come to you directly from God. Bear them lovingly, in a spirit of penance and mortification. He prefers that to all you can do of yourself.

That you have to endure these moments of discouragement is part of the Cross. You must not be surprised at these times of trial. We often fall as we carry our cross, but we must rise up again bravely.

You will acquire more merit in five minutes by patiently bearing suffering which God allows to come upon you, than by all the self-chosen mortifications you can do.

The mortifications which we can do of ourselves are nothing; they are the merest trifles and their value comes solely from the union of our acts with the will of God, and from the love which inspires us to do them for Him. From the moment we act outside His will, all we do is absolutely value-less.

Accept bravely the cross which God is giving you. It might be very much more painful, for you at least have the consolation of knowing that this trial will not offend God and is serving to sanctify your soul. If at times you think you are failing in submission and confidence, do not be troubled, for that is a trial inherent in the cross, it is the wood whereof it is made. Our Lord understands and forgives. Offer your pain in union with that of the blessed Virgin at the foot of the Cross, and by her hands.

Abandon

Accept trials from the hands of our Lord and see in the consolation He sends you the proof of His merciful tenderness.

It is up to us to accept with promptness and complete submission the dispositions of Providence, seeing the will of God in all things.

Do not worry about the shrinking you feel from suffering. Did our Lord in the Garden of Gethsemane rejoice at the thought of suffering? You ought to say, 'I accept, O Lord, with Your grace, this suffering, in absolute conformity to Your will'.

Offer to God your daily trials and annoyances: those little crosses which are sometimes harder to bear than the great ones. When you have done this, think no more about it.

When we have to bear some trial or suffering, if we were to think of the eternal sufferings we really deserve, we would see how small it really is. The sacrifices of this life are nothing, since everything passes away.

You are wrong in thinking that *abandon* means indifference when faced with suffering. Where would be the merit if we felt nothing? As long as you live, you will feel suffering and sorrow when trials come. When we suffer it does not mean we have not surrendered ourselves to God. It is enough that, notwithstanding all your shrinking, your will accepts. Even complaints are not a sin, provided that the intention whereby you accepted the will of God is not withdrawn. To fail there, a deliberate and contrary act of your will would be necessary.

How different my life has been from what I had hoped for! God's will be done!

We must never expose ourselves to temptation, because alone we should not be able to resist. On the other hand, when God permits a trial we must not doubt His help for a single moment.

I recommend myself to Almighty God and I lovingly accept death when and how God shall will in expiation of my sins, and I adore His divine decree.

Mortification

We must practise mortification in *Faith*, submitting our intelligence to believe revealed truth which we cannot understand, we must practise it in *Hope*, overcoming our fears and anxieties for the love of God and hoping for all from Him; we must practise mortification in *Love*, striving to be charitable in thought and act.

As far as possible practise interior mortification, which is the more necessary and without which the exterior is nothing.

Seek to mortify your will, yielding to that of others and anticipating the wishes of those around you; renouncing what you like; abstaining from saying what would turn to your advantage. Avoid always justifying yourself and having the last word.

We must not dread too much the annoyances and sufferings which may come from busying ourselves about our neighbour and trying to do him good. We cannot avoid sacrifices and trials for life is full of them, but the sacrifices and sufferings which are borne for the sake of this world are without merit and profitless for eternal life, whereas those we make to help our neighbour, in order to please God, gain merit which will have its reward in heaven.

The Giving of Self – Union with God

Offer yourself to God to fulfil His will, in union with the blessed Virgin and by her hands. Every morning, and when you go to Communion, renew this offering of yourself, asking Him to enable you to accept everything which He may will to send you. You must not worry about it, but only abandon yourself to God's good pleasure.

What you must aim at is the giving of yourself. This gift of self consists in accepting our Lord as absolute master in everything. You must submit yourself unreservedly to His will over your person and over all that affects you in soul or body, in the present and in the future. You must be nothing but a servant, a member and an instrument, led by our Lord alone. Your gifts, your virtues, your works, your actions, your sufferings must be for Him alone.

Let God lead you on gently, day by day, with great confidence in His mercy and His love for you.

It is not by minute self-examination that you will come to know yourself, but only by the grace of our Lord. If you ask Him for it He will give it to you.

Your outward life must contribute to the growth of your inner life; that is to say, you must so act that exterior circumstances serve to increase your union with God and not to dissipate you; serve you as instruments of virtue, not as occasions of sin.

Have the most steadfast hope in God's infinite goodness and mercy. All goodness comes from Him.

God will never let Himself be outdone in generosity. He plans for us according to His great mercy. He knows our weakness and how to pity it.

Prostrate yourself at the feet of our Lord with humility and love, showing Him your weakness, your poverty, your nothingness.

You must not be upset and worry yourself when God's hand seems to disappear, when like the Magi you lose sight of the star. Without changing everything, bravely follow the road marked out. If we faithfully practise obedience, we always find Jesus again.

Hope for everything from the infinite mercy of God. He

will find excuses for your sins. Jesus is not on the watch to punish you; He died to redeem you.

Never fear that our Lord will forsake you. *Corpus Christi* reminds us of that expression of His infinite tenderness: 'Behold, I am with you always, to the close of the age'. By His abiding Eucharistic Presence Jesus makes us see that He is ever with us. Why then should you fear that He abandon you?

Be very grateful to our Lord for all the countless tokens of His goodness which He has shown you. Think how every good thought, every aspiration, every prayer, every act of love, is a grace you owe to the Precious Blood which He shed for you. How great then should be your gratitude for all that He suffered and merited for you! The graces He grants you were bought by His pain, His humiliation, His death.

Open your heart to hope, even when, and especially when, you feel yourself urged in the contrary direction.

Cling to our Lord when you are frightened, keep yourself united to Him, fearing nothing, and thus wait until the storm passes.

Ask God for the grace of holy joy. Sadness comes from considering too much the world and its anxieties. Let your heart be warmed by the thought of the eternal joys and in the peaceful acceptance of sufferings which last such a little while and then pass away.

Do not be frightened by the devil's attempts to trouble you and rob you of your peace. Despise his efforts, trusting in the power and help of your Saviour and His blessed Mother. Let the matter drop and attach no importance to it. In time of temptation do not do as did St Peter, who, having ceased to keep his eyes fixed upon Jesus in order to look at the waves, began to sink. Keep your eyes fixed on our Lord.

The more we advance in age, the more does our Lord detach us from this earth, breaking the ties which bind us to this quickly fleeting life.

I do so wish that you would manage to be more tranquil, to despise the play of your imagination and rest in our Lord's arms. You are so near Him in solitude and He is at your side. I told you to forestall these trials and anxieties, to accept them joyfully before they take possession of your spirit. You will thus rob them of all their bitterness and you will have gained much merit.

Very often they will be 'Abraham's sacrifices' (a French expression wherein the will is taken for the deed), for, as you know, many of your fears are unfounded and, in the event, God does not ask the sacrifice you dread.

The will and the love of God are one and the same thing. They are the basis of the decrees of His Providence. Therefore you ought to be very obedient to the will of God. He will arrange all for our good. Life and death are in His hands. Never doubt His goodness. Everything which may happen will always be for your good. In order that your prayers may be heard you must abandon yourself to His will with the trustfulness of a child.

Confidence

Trust in the tender love of our Lord, which is greater than anything you can imagine. You will never be able to fathom the tenderness of the love He bears you.

Never doubt the tenderness of the Heart of Jesus. We have offended Him, grieved Him, but He holds out His arms to forgive us and press us to His Heart. The devil would have us condemned, but Jesus saves us by His Cross.

God is our Father. From all eternity He has carried us in His arms.

God loves you far more than a mother loves her little one.

You should reject every narrow, fearful thought, and not get a wrong idea of the meaning of detachment. You should be grateful to God for the graces He gives you and try to profit by them. You must not torment yourself with the fear that these graces will be withdrawn. Not having the grace for that at the present moment, you could not accept it as you ought. It is like martyrdom, for which God gives the strength at the moment when it is required. For the rest you must always believe that whether God gives or takes away, it is always in love.

The feast of the Blessed Sacrament recalls the most perfect manifestation of the love of Jesus for us. It is the Sacrament of His love, whereby He gives us testimony of His unchanging tenderness.

Banish fear from your heart, or rather let it be only fear engendered by love, full of the tenderness of a child towards its father.

Trustfulness, the attitude of the soul face to face with God, ought to be like that of a child towards its mother. It knows that she loves it, that she thinks of it, wills it good, that she will give it everything she deems necessary. But the mother also cannot always grant the child what it wants. Knowing that the thing would be harmful to it, she will not give the reason of her refusal, and the child does not on that account doubt its mother's love.

Like the child we must express our desires to God, pray to Him, ask Him for what we want from Him. If a child were never to ask its mother for anything, she would think that it did not set great store by her, that it did not count on her love for it. Often a child is so persistent in its demands, and so sure of obtaining what it hopes for, that it constrains its mother to give way. So God allows Himself to be moved by prayer and confidence.

Perhaps we may leave Jesus: He will never leave us.

He did not forsake us when we offended Him. He waited for us lovingly.

He will not forsake us now that, by His grace, we are His. He says to us: 'My child, do not doubt of my love. I will stay with you; trust me'.

Never lose confidence. The most terrible wound we can inflict on the Heart of Jesus is to doubt His forgiveness.

Let your trustfulness be full of joy and simplicity.

God is infinite justice, but He is also infinite mercy. There is no attenuation of our responsibility, no indulgence that we ourselves can conceive, whereof His fatherly love has not thought, and which He will not use towards us before judging us.

Do not be discouraged by failures. If you fail simply admit that you have failed. Then begin to do better, bravely and perseveringly, without seeking excuses whereby to justify yourself.

You must not be afraid that our Lord is weary of you, but you should draw ever nearer to Him by love of the Cross. Then he will unite you more closely to Himself.

Remember that Jesus is the priest *par excellence*. He may permit that we do not have the help of religion at death, but He is near us. You need never fear that He will forsake you at the hour of death.

Devotion to our Lady and the Saints

After already having given us everything, Jesus gave us His mother. Through the intercession of Mary He offers us a means of obtaining new graces. Let us turn confidently to her, and ask her for the grace to be faithful until death.

Every time we say the Hail Mary, let us really beg our Lady to intercede for us and help us at the hour of death.

The greater your devotion to the blessed Virgin, the closer will you be to our Lord.

From our Lady learn to practise charity towards your neighbour, lovingly and in forgetfulness of self.

Remember the virtues our Lady practised by pondering in her heart the words of our Lord. Ask for the grace to know how to preserve God's words lovingly in your heart, and that they may not lie sterile there.

As Mary took our Lord to St John, so try to give Jesus to those who come to you. Try to make Him known, to make Him loved. Do not be discouraged at feeling yourself unworthy.

God sometimes makes use of the poorest and lowliest instruments. Whilst humbling ourselves to nothing before Him, we should yet recognize what He asks and offer ourselves to carry it out.

Learn to set your hopes on heaven. Ask our Lady to obtain for you the grace of a trusting heart which does not allow itself to be downcast by daily trials. Lift up your heart to God, for worrying is harmful to your spiritual life.

Ask our Lady for the grace of humility. It was by her great humility that she found favour with God.

Ask our Lady to safeguard the purity of your conscience,

then you will have nothing to fear. Ask her to help you to fulfil your family duties so that you may always fulfil the will of God.

Think often of our Lady at the foot of the Cross. Unite your pain with hers; ask her to keep you pure of heart. It was because she was so pure that she suffered with so great a love.

During the days of Holy Week your place should be at the foot of the Cross, on Calvary beside our blessed Lady. If the darkness which surrounds you hides Jesus from your sight, think how she also could no longer see Him then. Nevertheless, she stayed by Him beneath the Cross. If you stay in the same place you will be very near His Heart.

The remembrance of the saints ought to encourage us, when we think how they had the same difficulties, the same struggles that we have, and that they are now in heaven for all eternity.

Ask St Joseph, who held Jesus in his arms so lovingly, to obtain you the grace to hold Him in your heart. May he protect you from every danger, by the love with which he protected the childhood of God! Ask him for the grace to accomplish your duties perfectly; first your duties as a Catholic, then those to your family and especially to your children.

Ask St Peter to keep alive in your heart the great gift of Faith. We think too little of being grateful for this grace of which so many are deprived. Thank God for this immense gift.

Pray to St Mary Magdalene to obtain for you from our Lord the grace to be wholly detached from everything which is not Himself. Pray that your heart may be free from every affection which does not lead to Him. Be generous in leaving all to follow Him.

Take St Mary Magdalene as your model. Meditate on her confidence and courage in overcoming human respect and contempt in order to go to Jesus. Be sure that she will likewise remove all the obstacles which hinder your going to Him.

Letters

Letters of Spiritual Direction

24 July 1898

Beloved Daughter in Christ,
You must be indulgent and forgive my long silence. I have just at this moment finished some unexpected additional work which has been occupying me, and I hasten to write a few lines to you in reply to your letter, which for many days now has been before me, reproaching me for the delay. I was sorry, too, not to have been able to see you before you left for Florence, but do not let us waste time lamenting this. I see that you are still a victim of that which threatens to become a chronic disposition – a tendency to lose courage – and you must combat this most energetically. It is a dreadful defect, not readily compatible with true humility, and therefore incompatible with genuine virtue. When will you learn that being unsuccessful is the only sure path for you? Success is a danger for the majority of people because few of them can bear the weight of it; for you it is a great danger. Your desire to succeed should not be other than the intention to do the best possible in the eyes of God. When you have done this, you have been successful. If this is afterwards followed by failure, at least outwardly, thank God for it because He is protecting you from the ruin which would probably ensue had you any reason to think well of yourself or be complacent about the successful outcome. Be sure then, after an apparent failure, to thank God for it, especially if this failure is accompanied by the ardent desire on your part to do better. You will gather from this that I do not intend to leave you in peace, sitting with your arms folded, but want

you to persevere. When you do not succeed, be glad of it
and thank God ...

Pray for me sometimes because I have need of help.

Devotedly in Christ ...

1911

Beloved Daughter in Christ,

I am sorry to think, my child, that I should have caused you
to feel shy and timid with regard to me. I hope I have not been
hard or unkind to you. If so, it was quite unintentional. I have
so often so many things on my mind, that sometimes I am
miles away in thought from what is going on about me, and I
am conscious that this must give the impression that I am
unapproachable and distant. You must not mind this weakness
or fault, but act and speak freely according to your mind.

Yours faithfully in Christ ...

20 July 1901

My dear Child,

I hasten to reply to your letter of the 18th instant. As I had
occasion to tell you *viva voce* after carefully considering the
reasons for and against, in my opinion you can scarcely doubt
that you have a vocation to the religious life. You have been
thinking about it already for a long time, and during these last
years you have had every chance to become acquainted with
the world and to sound your own feelings about a different
decision. It seems to me both useless and detrimental to
prolong this period of transition any further. The reasons
which you give for believing in a special call from God appear
valid to me, and if by chance, a thing I do not think probable,
they are not as firmly founded as I think at the moment, then
the novitiate will make you know for certain, and you will
know what to do once and for all. You tell me that someone

has suggested that you have not a true vocation, that it is merely a 'fixation'? For my part I do not see how anyone can have a vocation without a firm resolve and a very firm will. The person suggests amusements and novels to distract you. What does this mean, other than to try by all possible means to make you lose the vocation which you may have? One could even succeed, by such methods, in distracting a professed religious, making her lose her interior recollection and gradually destroying her vocation. There are plenty of religious who would be exposed to such a danger were they thrown back into the world into which God has not called them. It would be even easier to make someone lose her vocation if she were only at the beginning of her religious life. A vocation is a gift from God, and is a grace. We do well to examine it for a reasonable length of time, the better to sound our own hearts and to recognize the truth of the vocation, but we should not push matters beyond their proper limits and so do all in our power to try and lose the grace which we believe we have received. One can put one's health to the test to find out one's strength, but I do not think anyone would dream of endangering his life in order to convince himself that he is really healthy. These are the thoughts which come to me on reading the objections raised, and you will see what I thought of the plan to distract you with amusements and novels. You did not leave College yesterday, and have not lacked the opportunity to put your resolution to the test within prudent limits. I do not see any need to wait any longer. It is quite obvious that you will have difficulties to surmount in the religious life, as do all who decide to embrace a life of sacrifice, but just because it is a state in which you have to labour to attain perfection, you must not imagine that you should already be perfect when entering the convent. I am sure that your parents, who do not wish other than your happiness, will not hesitate to make this sacrifice, the merit of which will be great in the eyes of God, and for which He will most certainly bless them. I pray our Lord both for them and for you, and bless you with all my heart.

My dear Child,

I was very eager to have your news and was pleased to receive your letter this morning, which has brought me up to date with all that has happened since you last wrote to me. If the question of the diploma had closed the door of the Society to you, I should not have hesitated to advise you to try elsewhere, but the fact that you have surmounted this difficulty would seem to indicate still more clearly that it is there that God wants you. I do understand perfectly how this last stage of the sacrifice you have to make of your legitimate affection makes you suffer, and I sympathize with all my heart. But if I can understand and sympathize with you, how much more must our Lord understand and open His compassionate Heart to you! Despite all your weakness, your fears and your repugnance, you are very close to Him at this time, but it is a kind of Calvary, and on Calvary one suffers without feeling any consolation and without interior enlightenment, but one loves with a pure and supernatural love which prepares one for the ineffable and eternal joy of the final union with God. Think of the holy Virgin at the foot of the Cross, and you will understand this. Suffering passes, to have suffered remains eternally. Take heart. All the people who give themselves to God have to pass through this period of testing, which both purifies and moulds our hearts. The more fully one gives oneself, the more one suffers. Our Lord is always at our side, and invites us to tell Him all our grief, to pour out our sorrow before Him so that He may bless us and help us. I pray for you every day and hope to see you again in ... and to help you while it is in my power to do so. Please remember me in your prayers ...

21 October 1904

My dear Child,
Please excuse me for using a typewriter but in this way I am able to write at least a few lines to you, to thank you for your letter, your good wishes and your prayers. Yes, above all, thank you for your prayers, because I have great need of them. At present I have so little time in which to pray but nonetheless try to make all my activities, my occupation and my anxieties a form of prayer. I am deeply pleased to learn that you are happy, and are happy because you seek all your joy in the love of our Lord. Take great care never to seek it elsewhere, not even in moments of trial. Then, above all, turn to our Lord because He is waiting for you in such moments to draw you more closely to Himself. What struck me especially about your retreat resolution was the decision you made not to fear committing faults and being corrected for them. That is the way to overcome self-love and to draw profit from your weakness. It goes without saying that this is not a question of being negligent or of encouraging a 'don't care' attitude, but it means that while doing all you can not to neglect your duties, you will have a holy liberty of spirit, carrying out your work energetically, with prudent and acceptable initiative. You will also have a thousand occasions for practising humility when you fall. The saints have acted thus and their faults and their mistakes became milestones in the path of perfection. Pray the good God a little that if it is His will and for His greater glory, I may soon be freed from the burden of this position and free to seek intimate union with Him in another way. I bless you from my heart and thank you once again . . .

1915

I felicitate you on the solitude and silence which have been reserved for you at this time. What could be more desirable or useful! And yet, in the life of a Sister of the Sacred Heart, rarely do external pressures allow such a privilege. So thank God for this. It is indeed a great grace that you are enabled to erect and guard your own 'Carmel'! When God allows us to be put aside on account of poor health or other circumstances, or left behind in the usual course of the active life which takes place around us, then indeed are we privileged! What ineffable joy, what peace without idleness, what an apostolate to exercise for souls in a life of prayer, living more interiorly in God and for God, growing in a spirit of prayer and self-abnegation! For then we exercise our mission without fear of hindering the work of God in us and in others through the mistakes we make in our external activity, which is frequently permeated by self-love and subtle self-seeking. Thank God for this time. I bless you with all my heart, and bless all your intentions.

1927

I received your letter of the 17th yesterday. I read and re-read it attentively and have considered all that you have confided to me. I have prayed about it and it does not seem difficult to me to reply because I can see clearly what I ought to say . . . As regards your sufferings, if they come from God, they are a profitable trial and a sign of His love. Therefore accept this trial willingly, close your eyes and go on moment by moment, entrusting yourself to God's mercy, without seeing, without questioning. Your virtue will thus be better based and more profitable than in times of consolation. Let Jesus work in your soul, as He pleases. Remain at His feet quite resigned and content that you are good for nothing . . .

My Child, do not even for a moment think of lessening the frequency of your Holy Communions. Indeed, the more you are suffering, the more you are in obscurity and afflicted, the more ought you to seek relief in the Eucharist, in which Jesus is awaiting you every day, even if He hides himself and is silent. Believe me, the trial which you are undergoing at this time is a means of sanctification and of the greatest benefit, a time of merit and a pledge of love. Be of good heart. If the Lord calls you to struggle in aridity and with little comfort, it is a sign that He will give you the strength to bear it.

Letters to Laity

1921

I should like to see you more resigned even in your legitimate cause for grief. Do not try to suffocate your heartache but to sanctify it with Jesus. You hold a treasure in your hands, the precious means of practising virtue in a most excellent way, so do not spoil it. Your grief is legitimate, but you should elevate it, transform it, and not suffocate it with merely human efforts. Otherwise you run the risk of staying alone with yourself, instead, as I should wish for you, of staying alone with Jesus. Do not feel sorry for yourself, hugging your grief to yourself, but gently offer everything to Jesus, begging Him to be your comfort, to help you to accept this sacrifice. Do not let yourself be dominated by your personal grief, by too frequently recalling all the particulars. I send you my blessing and am praying for you.

25 June 1917

This is perhaps indiscreet of me, but after reading your letter, I feel I want to tell you something. This morning in Chapel I was looking at the little light which burns before the most holy Sacrament and noticed the wick. At times it splutters, flares, smokes and smoulders. It does not always burn well and is consumed almost without giving any light. Nobody bothers with it and for many hours nobody even looks at it. Neither does one appreciate its usefulness when it is compared with other more beautiful candles, or one sees it beside fresh flowers, golden candlesticks and precious vases. However, who would dare to say that it is really a useless thing? One can well do without all the rest but not without this little light while it is fulfilling its modest function, composed of fidelity and constancy, a sign of Love which is imperfect, certainly, but is never refused. Love which appears to have little to recommend it but which is more appreciated by the Lord than other more attractive and easily admired gifts – I thought of you: perhaps I was not wrong in so doing, and I believe Jesus would agree with me. He looks at the heart, and knows how to sympathize with our wretchedness and appreciate the modest efforts of our good will. I bless you from my heart.

Letters to His Beloved Boys in Wartime

November 1916

I have just learned that you have been injured, seriously injured. This had greatly saddened me and I am writing to you to assure you of my sympathy. You have done your duty most nobly and about this I am deeply pleased, but my grief is great when I think of what you have suffered and are still suffering.

I do not know where you are and I am not able to help you. But if there is something I can do today or tomorrow, you must let me know.

I am praying more than ever for you and your family and trust that the Lord will comfort and heal you.

Monsignor also sends his greetings. I bless you with sincere affection.

1 January 1918

Dear Virgilio,
In the hope that these lines will reach you, I am writing to tell you that I am thinking of you, and wishing to bring you some comfort. We have been in the greatest anxiety for some time because we had no news of you, and not knowing your fate, we feared the worst.

You will understand the anguish of your mother and father. I had the joy of giving them the news of your safety and it has been an immense relief for them. Now there remains the sorrow of knowing that you are a prisoner and perhaps deprived of everything. Today your mother gave me your letter of 2nd December to read. She has already posted some parcels but does not know if they have arrived yet. It is not possible for her at this time to send all that she would like to since regulations in this matter are explicit and necessarily restrictive; but everything which is possible will be done.

I have asked the Nuncio at Munich, Monsignor Pacelli, to take an interest in you, and especially to provide for your needs if he can. I have authorized him to purchase whatever is useful or necessary.

But your mother and your father are well, and we often see each other. Naturally the subject of our conversations is always Virgilio.

All your companions in the Association are concerned about you and frequently talk about you most affectionately, as they do about all the others at the Front. Unfortunately we have heard nothing from some of them since last October and have reason to fear that they have fallen ... Please God that they, too, are safe.

Berni has just returned injured, but not seriously.

Do not lose heart. Take care of your health as far as possible and put yourself into the hands of the Lord! I hope you are not forced into complete idleness. However, you know that we do not forget you and we are close to you in thought.

I am praying for you, entrusting you to the Sacred Hearts of Jesus and Mary, and I bless you with sincere affection.

Letters to a Convert

I cannot but believe that our friendship was intended by God
for a set purpose, and I trust as a means of helping you to
know better and to embrace that which you have loved almost
without knowing it – His truth. I am at a loss to explain otherwise an unexpected meeting and the warm feeling of friendship which seemed to exist between us from the first moment
I saw you. As we left the Scots College together and walked
down the street, I felt as if I had always known you and as if
it were the most natural thing in the world that we should be
talking as we did ... So far nothing that you have done or
suffered has been useless, either for yourself or for others, but
it would be so the day you turn away from what you clearly
see and cease to follow His gentle guidance. That will never
be, I hope, and He will reward the good you have done by
bringing you to the peace His truth alone can give. Suffering
is indeed a grace, or perhaps I should say a channel of grace
... You will pray, won't you? I cannot tell you how deeply
convinced I am that all is there. No books, no thought or argu-
ment, however powerful, can avail without prayer. I wish I
could tell you how often I have experienced it, but you know
this as well, or better than I do. Need I say that I will pray
and get prayers for you?

I have no experience of what your life is, and it is difficult
for me to picture it for myself ... I do not think there is
anything profane in your remarks that one could love God
more if one understood Him better. Indeed, that is quite true,
for love is intelligent, especially when it is divine, and it must
rest on knowledge. The better we understand and realize how
good and loving He is to us, the more we feel our hearts burn
with love for Him. The world does not love Him because the
world 'knew Him not'. There are degrees in the knowledge
and therefore in the love. It is in heaven we love God perfectly
and permanently, because it is there that we contemplate Him
face to face with unveiled and perfect vision, and know as we
are known ... I say this precisely because I know that you
cannot love God as you ought, nor love Him constantly, nor
have the happiness and peace and rest which that love gives,

without knowing and understanding God – God's truth in all its beauty – by faith, and under veils – that knowledge of God which in heaven is unveiled. The vision of the blessed is but the development, the result, the crown of the life of faith here on earth. And the life of faith means a living faith, a life of grace and sanctity. Faith is indeed a grace, it does not exclude, but presupposes study and intelligent consideration of the motives of credibility. That study, that labour, accompanied by prayer, will deserve the crowning grace of faith as its reward. I certainly do and will pray for you, that you may no longer be beaten about in uncertainty or only be favoured with glimpses of the truth that come and go, and which no doubt involve a responsibility and a duty, but upon them you cannot rest a love of God which should be permanent and unshaken, and foreshadow the fixedness of the love in Heaven. Would you mind very much if I were to suggest a 'Hail Mary' said every night for the above intention? Or are you of those who strangely think or feel that Mary stands between their hearts and God? I trust not. He who is all Truth and Life and Light gave Himself to the world in the Incarnation through the instrumentality of Mary, and so it is that He is often pleased to give Himself to us individually and communicate the graces of the Redemption to our souls through her intercession. But many close the door on Mary, like the people of Bethlehem on Christmas night, and hence our Lord is not born under their roof . . .

There should be no haste, no suddenness, I was almost going to say no sentiment, in making up your mind, in working out your conviction. Nothing could be more harmful. You must take your time, and discuss the bearings of the whole question. But the day you are convinced, and when your mind is made up – after considering all the issues, then indeed delay would be dangerous. You must act at once; suddenness and haste become a duty. Your fear of a possible reaction seems to point to the absence, as yet, of complete conviction, unless you are struggling unawares against conviction . . .

I do not think that this state will last very long. I hope and pray that it may soon give place to rest and peace through the truth. You are right to speak of the change of religion as the 'so-called change of religion' for one there can only be. In your case, especially, I can't help thinking that the only change there will be is that, after having loved what you did not know, you come to know what you have loved.

There is something very painful to me at the thought of how terribly lonely and restless you must feel at times. I long to see you in the light and joy which would make all the world home to you. God bless and keep you through all this trying time . . .

I received your letter with joy, but I could not read it without sadness. I often pray for you – somehow you are constantly in my thoughts, even in the midst of engrossing work. If I were with you as often as I remember you and pray to God to lead you on 'O'er moor and fen, o'er crag and torrent till the night is gone' you would not often be alone.

I shall pray to God to guide you through these last stages. I feel deeply for you in the necessity of causing pain to others . . . Be full of trust. It will all come right.

Your letter fills me with joy. I have been thinking of you so much and looking forward to the great event for your sake. What a memorable Holy Week this has been for you, and what a glorious Easter! I am busy thanking God for His goodness to you.

On Friendship

God gives us the pleasure of seeing our friends, and of enjoying their company when he thinks fit, as in His Fatherly love He gives us many other human comforts, for we are His children. Why not take those comforts as such from His hands, enjoy them, and bless Him for the joy? Naturally, when they cease, we cannot fail to experience regret or sorrow; were it otherwise we should not be human . . . Our readiness to give up our friends at any moment in spite of pain, as and when God pleases, willingly and joyfully – to bless Him equally in the joy and in the sorrow – is where perfection lies, and it is the means of utilizing all these gifts to His greater glory, and of proving our love for Him. Our detachment is what counts, and detachment is in the will, controlling and schooling our feelings. But if we do not feel – in joy or sorrow – what is there to control, to offer up, to sanctify, to use for God? He is our Father, above all things our Father. If He gives us joy, let us rejoice in it for His sake; when He withdraws it, let us rejoice again, even in sorrow, because we can make a gift to Him, and a gift that costs us something.

Spiritual Insights

You speak of your path being one of 'humiliation and solitude' but 'very simple and straight' and you set yourself the question, 'Why are there any interior struggles?' Your answer strikes me as somewhat severe, 'a want of generosity'. Perhaps that is part of the explanation, for we are rarely generous enough; but I am inclined to think that it is not all. First there is the reluctance of our *natural* weakness to earn our heavenly bread in the sweat of our brow, and inevitable fatigue. Then there is the tendency to seek the abiding city here below and hurry in our desire to reach final and perfect peace. Yet what should we do without these struggles? They are the material with which we build up our spiritual edifice and our interior life, they are the rungs of the ladder which we have to climb; they are the rocks which we must strike to bring forth the waters of divine love. Nor can we hope or wish to avoid them whilst we are in the flesh. Only in eternity, in complete union with God, is there real and unchanging *life*; only there can we *live*, that is to say, live fully without obstacles, without weakness and hence without struggles. On this side of the grave we can only live imperfectly; there are numberless trammels and unavoidable conflicts from within and without. Our life must ever be a kind of constant death. If able to say in that sense *quotidie morimur* it is a happiness. For in the measure in which we *die* to the things of this world, to interior and exterior obstacles, in that degree may we be said to *live*, for we begin to possess something of the perfect *life* in eternity, God. We must either die to the world and ourselves, or die to God. If we were to die to God, we might perhaps enjoy the world to a certain extent and for a time, but we should enter eternity dead to God and eternal life. Whereas if we die to the world and to ourselves according to our powers, we *live* to God, and living we shall step into eternity to share the perfect life of God. That is, I take it, what is implied in the mystical death of which the saints have spoken, and it seems to be conveyed in our Lord's words: 'He that loveth his life shall lose it, and he that hateth his life in this world keepeth it unto life eternal'. But it is hard to die, and struggle there must be. Sudden deaths are not frequent. I have let my pen run on and I fear I may have written confusedly about what you know already and better than I do. However, as I have scribbled so much I had better send these lines as they are . . .

Speeches

Speech to the Seminarians of the North American College
(Rome, 6 August 1921)

Your good Rector has suggested that I address you this morning, and I am very glad to do so; but I do not think that I can say what you have not heard before, nor can I say in a better way what others have said before me. Moreover, he suggested that I take as my inspiration the famous exhortation of Pius X to his clergy, written some thirteen years ago.

This exhortation is a wonderful proof of His Holiness' great love for his priests, and he intended that it should be a constant guide, a *Vade mecum*, for them. It was my privilege to be at his side at that time, and I watched him write almost every word of it. He worked at it for three weeks, and amidst his almost crushing occupations he yet found time to read portions of it to me every morning as he was writing it. His purpose was to raise the standards of the Catholic priesthood. Although most of you are not yet ordained, but yet since you hope to be priests, I shall speak to you as priests; and surely it is not too soon to enter into the spirit of the priesthood.

If I may be permitted a personal reminiscence, let me tell you of a good Irish priest that took trouble over me when I was a boy, talked to me, taught me my Catechism, and so forth. I still have the letters that he wrote, and when writing he always used the words 'we priests'. 'We priests' should do this, 'we priests' should do the other things; 'we priests' should avoid this, 'we priests' should avoid the other thing. I was but a boy of ten at the time, but he knew that I would like and hoped to be a priest, and his words always rang in my ears.

The Holy Father compiled those pages with tender love.

And if every priest and cleric had that treatise in his hands, and, in the busy life which affords little opportunity for other studies, would peruse a little of it from day to day, he would serve God as he ought. What is the purpose which His Holiness had in mind and which underlies the whole work? I take it that it was this: that we who are set apart for the service of God are bound to foster the spiritual life and to be guided in all our thoughts, in all our words and in all our actions by considerations of a supernatural character. In the natural order of things, all advantages and attractions end with this world; whereas our life with God remains and is immortal. Everybody is rushing after material advantages as if this world were the end of everything. We breathe in this atmosphere and we must acknowledge that priests are apt to fall down to that level, and instead of raising souls up, they themselves are dragged down to the level of those whom they pretend and desire to elevate. Nothing could be more opposed to God's interests.

This is what Pius X was aiming at: to help us to attain that high standard of spiritual life which ought to be found in a priest. St Paul calls it a holy priesthood, and he calls us 'partakers of a heavenly vocation'. 'Holy brethren, partakers of the holy vocation, consider the apostle and the high priest of our confession, Jesus' (*Ad Heb.*). St John Chrysostom calls it the 'vestment of Christ'. In the Old Law, in the beginning, the first born of every family was set apart for the priesthood; later, the priests were chosen from the tribe of Levi alone. Certainly the priesthood of the Old Law was a great and holy dignity, but it does not compare at all with the New. Yet people who do not look at it from the supernatural standpoint consider it a respectable profession, useful for the people, and think that it should be maintained for the benefit of the commonweal. We cannot afford to take this idea of the Holy Priesthood. We should never lose sight of the fact that we are endowed with an awful power, a power that brings down from heaven the spotless Lamb of God, and by which the Precious Blood of our Lord floods the earth from pole to pole, bringing life, joy and happiness to the world. This sublime privilege should be constantly before our eyes, a privilege that has not been granted to the angels, and before which our Blessed Lady herself, the Mother of God, stands in holy awe. And that other power, the power over the Mystical Body of Christ, the power of breaking the bonds of Satan and raising up souls from the mire of sin and making them as pure almost as the angels of heaven. Oh, how every dignity of this world vanishes and becomes small and even despicable in the sight of the priesthood of God! Oh, the iniquity of forgetting our powers and responsibilities and of not accepting the duties that are laid upon us!

How are we to provide for this supernatural habit of mind whether in success or in failure? There the Holy Father tells us what has been said again and again but never too often. He tells us that above all other things stands prayer. He traces out what form our prayers should take. I am not speaking of vocal prayer, keep this before your mind. It is necessary, we all know; but I am speaking of the spirit that must animate our prayers, and without which our prayers become mere lip-worship. St Paul says that we must pray always. It is evident that he does not refer to vocal prayer. We cannot always be saying our beads. '*Cum potes,*' says St Augustine, '*ore lauda, cum non potes corde lauda, corde benedic, corde in aram conscientiae victimas sacras impone*'. Praise with thy lips when able to do so, but if unable – and therefore more frequently and constantly – praise and bless Him with thy heart and place sacred holocausts upon the altar of thy heart. These holocausts are the restrictions that we have to place upon ourselves almost hourly in order to preserve us from sin and as a safeguard of our sacred office. And this constitutes an habitual prayer. We cannot afford to indulge unrestrictedly in the freedom allowed to those who are not consecrated to God. We are in the world, but not of the world. Hence we have to give up many things, legitimate in themselves and which others can enjoy. We cannot live as seculars. This is undoubtedly a sacrifice for human nature and a prayer because it is a sacrifice. We must guard our hearts, our thoughts, our affections, that they may never be aught else but the thoughts, the affections of a priest. However much we happen to be engrossed in outward things, absorbed in the work we have in hand, however numerous and varied the duties that

we are obliged to attend to, when our time is not our own and
countless calls are distracting our attention in behalf of others,
and are preventing us from granting a thought to ourselves – yes
even then our habit of prayer should be such that there be ever
within our hearts a hidden corner, a guarded sanctuary where
we can always seek refuge, where we can always find God, and
where God can find us. If this spirit of prayer is ours, we shall
never cease to enjoy the presence of God. Not we, but He will
be doing our work. We shall be powerful *'in opere et sermone'*.
This supernatural view and this spirit of prayer will permeate
our work in the ministry and render it really fruitful: fruitful in
the sight of God. St Augustine also says: *'In innocentia operum
tuorum prepara animam tuam ad laudandum Deum tota die.
Quidquid egeris, bene age, et laudasti Deum'*. If we do everything from the supernatural standpoint we really make God our
companion and thus we cannot lose contact with Him. God does
not ask of us our words but our hearts.

Many think that sanctity consists in accomplishing things
which attract the eyes of men. These things are necessary and
oftentimes good for the Church, but this is not sanctity. Sanctity must be within us. How many humble priests there are in
distant missions who are considered as inferiors, but who are
higher in the sight of God in sanctity that those who seem to
be on the pinnacle. God does not measure things from the
human standard, and if we have the supernatural point of view
we will never be discouraged. If we make sacrifices joyfully,
and not in a half-hearted way, even the greatest trial will be a
pleasure. This is the supernatural standpoint, and if we take it
we will not be crushed by humiliations and mortifications.

And again – I will be frank with you, for we can speak of
such things here among ourselves – superiors are not infallible; they are human and sometimes make mistakes. They
may even commit injustices, though always, I hope, unwit-
tingly. But if they do seem hard to get along with, let us suffer
it willingly from the hand of God and see God in them and in
the trials He sends us. That is the supernatural view.

We must carry the light of Jesus Christ to our fellow
country-men. The supernatural light seems to be carried away
by the world, but that light will never be carried away. I urge

you, therefore, to take this point of view that you may live on supernatural principles not theoretically but practically. Then your life will be happy, useful and prosperous. God does not ask you to be great if He does not give you the opportunity or the ability. If you are always governed by supernatural principles, every word you speak and every gesture you make will have weight and will lead to God.

Each and every one of you should have a copy of this famous exhortation, and each and every one of you should read a page or two of it every day. Make it your *Vade mecum* and it will accompany you through life and admonish you as a voice behind your back. It is the voice of one who was always an exemplary priest even amidst trials and contradictions. It is the voice of one whom – no matter what defects or mistakes his adversaries may have sought to find in him or his actions – everybody admitted to have been above all a true priest. And if we can meet with the same eulogy, we shall have run a good race, and we will have been good and faithful servants. Let us be priests, really good and earnest priests, for one good priest alone can save a nation. And then, too, we will receive the crown of glory which our Lord promises to all those who are good and faithful to Him. Amen.

Speech to the International League of Catholic Women
(May 1922)

Only five days ago I received your invitation to preside at your meetings, and it arrived whilst I was particularly busy. I admit to having tried to find a reason to decline, not because I was not interested in your great cause, because I am, but because I had no time to prepare, and felt that I would let you down. Then the Holy Father asked me to help you, and when your own members prevailed upon me again, I had no option but to accept with the best will in the world.

But what is much more important than this is the fact that I bring you the blessing of the Vicar of Christ, of Pope Pius XI, who in his great wisdom and apostolic zeal takes a particularly pronounced interest in the success of all your efforts.

I also bring with me – I hope it is appropriate for me to mention this – the echo of the great and holy former pontiff's warm support, since Pope Pius X was most paternally interested in your cause from the moment you first began. None of us has forgotten him.

The apostolate you have chosen – and there is no other more fitting word to describe your labours – has an incontestable importance. It seems to me that you are equal to the task. You are called to assist in the construction of a truly Christian society. This task is now urgent, and as every day goes by we have more proof of this urgent need.

You are much better placed to be effective than many other leagues for women which do not have any formal association with the Church, no matter what their objectives, what the talents of those involved, no matter how many resources of any kind they have at their disposal. You have no need to go out hunting desperately for new doctrines, all of which will result in shipwreck, as we see from those poor souls who fall feverishly into this trap, propelled by imprudence and mere enthusiasm.

No. Inspired by the Faith and with a solid foundation in the immortal principles of the Gospel and the divine teachings taught by the only true teaching authority, the Petrine Office and the true shepherd of souls, the pope, your leagues have a mission. It is to study and to put into practice these doctrines in accordance with the needs and demands of our own century: *Nova et Vetera*.

You have at your disposal a large freedom of spirit by virtue of the fact that you have permission to confront in all honesty the grave problems of our day which must be resolved, armed with the teachings of an undisputed authority, which has been entrusted to us by God so that truth can be taught and diffused throughout the whole world.

It is your job to raise the standard of Christ. You know that you are bound to reconcile the duties with the rights of each woman, neither over-emphasizing nor undermining either. You will be doing everything to protect woman, so that she is not robbed of her aura, the aura of her dignity as a woman, defending the order established by Divine Providence, so that she does not fall off her pedestal and start to compete with men, becoming their virtual enemies, rather than the enlightened companion God created her to be, with a mission and a world of her own influence, namely the home. You will be doing everything to prevent her from becoming the base plaything of others, the object of their passions, glorified for as long as she can attract and entertain, but cast aside the next day by the very people who had transformed her into a victim of their own caprices.

Whilst giving due attention to special circumstances and individual cases, you will defend womankind against all the deceptive trends that go hand in hand with a morality which excludes or denies God, which tend to uproot woman from the family home where she belongs quite naturally and where she resides as a queen. To destroy the family home, which is the sacred and inviolate cell of all human society, and above all of Christian society, is the death-knell of civilization.

If we glance at your conference agenda we can see the importance of all the subjects you have chosen to consider. First and foremost, it is your desire to preserve and propagate the Faith. After the First World War society was in turmoil, for obvious reasons, but the turmoil continued in the moral sphere, which is why the work of teaching the Faith must have pride of place. We know for a fact that the current turmoil is a direct consequence of ignorance of the teachings of the Church. Never forget, dear Ladies, that it is not Christianity which has failed or has been found wanting; rather the problem is the fact that Christianity has started to genuflect and lose its vigour in the face of a new wave of paganism. Some assimilate the new paganism without realizing it. Others preach and glorify it as if it were an idol to be revered. So today we remind ourselves of what is true. The only way of finding true happiness is to revive the principles of the Faith which has saved the world.

Our danger is less the enemy which has, as it were, openly declared its hostility to Us, treating us with disdain and contempt. Rather it is the less apparently wicked monster we can call 'rationalism'. Sooner or later the spirit of rationalism seems to colonize all forms of modern Protestantism, it pene-

trates all the new religious systems, all lay schools of morality. That spirit insinuates lies. It implies that truth and error,
and good and evil are no more than purely subjective cat-
egories, which have the right to coexist with truth on the same
footing.

I add my voice to that of Fr De Ravignan, a great French
orator, who famously said that we now have the proverbial
'enemy within'. We have people who claim to be Christian,
even Catholic, but who are caught up in a web of illusions and
arbitrary speculations, and who concoct their own ideas about
religion and Christianity to suit their own lights.

What does he have to say, in his prophetic voice? That one
day in the future we will have a kind of Christianity which
proclaims that Christianity has outlived itself, and is dead.
There may be the vestiges of a teaching here or there, it will
not really matter. What will be characteristic will be the indifference to absolute, revealed truth. People will no longer
believe that truth can be pinpointed. They will allege that
everything about truth is generically elusive. There will no
longer be objectively binding duties and obligations. Rather
souls will dip into what flatters and caresses them, nothing
more than vague religious feeling will hold sway, and it will
be no more or less the play-thing of the fluctuations of character, temperament and skeptical rationalism. There will be no
solidity, no purpose, no fruits.

In this connection we do well to remember what the Church
has always taught about mixed marriages and all kinds of inter-
confessionalism. You will then be able to do justice to your
subject of the morality of cinema, theatre, fashion and dancing.

All people at this point in history, in government or elsewhere, who at least take their duties seriously, are preoccu-
pied and concerned about the decline in standards and the
outbreak of frenetic passion at all levels of society, the quest,
at any cost, for pleasure, entertainment and excitement, and
the slow but steady degeneration – possibly leading to the ultimate destruction – of the species, man. His spirit is literally
being sapped dry of all the nourishment it needs to survive.
The prospect inspires shame in us, as we reflect upon what is
happening around us.

How ironic, then, that whilst the police resort to certain measures to keep alcoholism and cocaine consumption under control, and apply the measure with strict severity, no-one seems to worry about the damage done to souls, the poison that has penetrated the soul, especially the souls of the young, bearing in mind that they are permitted to devour avidly all sorts of films, watch all sorts of plays, and to flaunt themselves shamelessly wearing shocking fashions, going to immodest dances.

We even have the topic of prostitution with all that that spells in terms of ruin. We must consider the civic duties of women too, the responsibilities and the dangers. All these issues are grave indeed. Whilst you will do your best to tackle them today, it is obvious that they will require further study before you can arrive at conclusions and make suggestions as to what practical measures can be adopted so that remedies will be effective.

I close expressing the hope and desire that the discussions you will be holding over the next few days will really bear fruit. That they most certainly will do, since you will all take it upon yourselves to control your purely personal desires and opinions, so that attention is brought firmly to bear on the topic in all its gravity and clarity. Retain your serenity as you debate and talk; bear the common good in mind, and never lose sight of it; think of the greatness of your cause, and how universally you are represented here, facing universal challenges.

Through the intercession of the Virgin Mother Mary, blessed amongst all women, may God guide you and bestow upon you all the joy of being able to see the fruits of your labours and sacrifices for such a great cause, which is as much our Lady's own cause, as it is the cause of Holy Mother Church.

**Speech to the Sixth Congress of the
International League of Catholic Women**
(*October, Holy Year 1925*)

My dear Ladies,
Holy Year has brought you all to the Eternal City where you
will be exchanging ideas with one another and sharing your
knowledge that you have acquired by dint of your labours in
the last period. You will be able to discuss the fruits of your
research, clarify what it is you are aiming for in the future,
coordinate as best you can all the means you have at your
disposal which will make your work in common more effective and efficacious. Above all, you are well placed to revive
your faith, placed as you are so close to the blessed tombs of
all the Apostles and Martyrs. Likewise you can implore the
Vicar of Christ for light and guidance in all your plans,
submitting to him, for his approval, all that you consider
necessary and useful in the way of your apostolate.

Welcome, dear Ladies, to this homeland for the soul;
remember you are being protected by the great Shepherd of
souls, the Roman pontiff; remember that the loyalty you have
to him and to your own immortal souls is not irreconcilable
with the love you have for your own countries. On the
contrary. Here you will also feel closer to your Heavenly
Home, to the promised land, which is the only worthwhile
goal, the only worthwhile aspiration of all souls. Both right
reason and the Faith tell us that all our affections must be
ordered to this highest of goals if those selfsame affections are
to retain their true nobility and their true efficacy.

Your task is both delicate and grave. I know that the
responsibilities which it entails are not lost on any of you.
Modern society imposes a myriad number of competing
demands on us, many of them insinuating, transitory and
contradictory. It is very difficult to reconcile all these
demands and to create a harmonious whole out of them, and
it is particularly difficult to harmonize them with the
immutable principles of the Catholic Faith, since in many
cases they are implicated in error; still more they are the

expression of a perplexing quest for excitement, diversion and light entertainment; there is the unapologetic quest for pleasure as an end in itself; there is resentment of the given duties of state and of the obligations which all Christians have to honour. There are many who seem to be devoted to purely temporal desires. They long for earthly fulfillment, for material riches and are so given over to these false friends that they forget that life is, by definition, a temporary affair. But how can they justify abandoning God, our sovereign good, true source of the only true happiness there is? And yet deference to divine law is the *sine qua non*.

We expect you to be receptive to evidence of human progress but at the same time we ask for discernment. You must never be as the 'blind leading the blind', accepting all that is new in a spirit of passivity, as if you were not expected to be vigilant about the proximate danger of error, vice, sin and the like. Remember that what is often billed as 'reform' and 'progress' is no more than a pretext to introduce yet more retrograde, reprehensible and deleterious signs of neopaganism.

You have no rights to abandon the citadel to the enemy, as it were, to haggle and bargain over truth, to envelop it in a seductive veil of error. Still less are you entitled to extinguish the light shining out of the lighthouse of Faith.

I am sure it is very wearying to have to work against the rising tide of all those fashionable trends and opinions which so bewitch souls, and so undermine the very basis of all Christian morality; I know, only too well, how difficult it is to dissect the propaganda of false, capricious doctrines which the masses fall for in utter, abject gullibility. We know how the appeal depends on stimulating the senses, on exciting the appetites, on undermining the necessity of restraint, of self-control, of self-government. We have been made in God's image, and given in nature and grace a certain capacity to protect ourselves from all the audacity of deregulated passions and vice. Shame and prudence can protect us from their aberrations, which is why you must highlight, before it is too late, the dangers posed by cooperating with these extraordinarily ferocious attacks. The seduction tactics are so insinuating now that virtually nothing is spared: childhood and innocence is at risk, so is the noble ideal of female education, so is the dignity of woman, of the family and of society. But resistance to evil and sin is now more important than ever before. The success of our antagonist is, as ever, only of limited duration, which is why you can fight on, embracing the ideal of heroism, of martyrdom and self-sacrifice for this great cause, of raising the standard of Christ amidst the ruins of Christian civilization.

You have taken a particular theme this year, 'the dangers which threaten the family and, as a result, society as a whole'. As the Cardinal-Protector of this venerable League I welcome the seriousness of your work, which is especially relevant to the challenges of today. For, if you acquire a greater vigilance in the course of studying how the enemy works, your work will have served a great and noble purpose. After all, it historically falls to woman to defend and protect the family. This is her sublime calling, indeed it is her mission. If woman fails in this her mission at home, society as a whole disintegrates. By undermining the unity, authority and morality of family life, society inevitably loses its vitality, and literally all its moral, physical and spiritual sources.

Even in terms of natural law alone the most intelligent men in the pagan era could see that this was true. They had not the light of revealed truth to guide them, but they too condemned the excesses which destroyed the basic unit in society. Only later was Christianity able to dispel their errors and envelop in supernatural truth what they had attempted to establish in purely natural terms, the human facts about the human condition.

I think one single example will illustrate this point well. Tacitus waxed lyrical about the domestic life of Agricola. What was it that so impressed him about Agricola's marriage? It was the fact that man and wife lived in harmony with one another, always seeking to find ways of making sacrifices for the beloved. *Invicem se anteponendo.* A marriage in which there is no subjection of wife to husband, and of children to the parents, is a marriage which leaves much to be desired, for if there is no visible hierarchy in a family, how will children know how to recognize the visible hierarchy in the

Church? If children are brought up to respect authority in the home, they will be able to discern the difference between duties, obligations and rights, and keep all in a healthy balance. *Invicem se anteponendo.*

When the concord between man and wife is animated by the divine breeze of supernatural grace and the law of charity, all tyranny and severity dissolves, all bitterness evaporates, all insubordination disappears. The spirit of revolt finds no home in such marriages. Rather, there is peace, the peace of Christ and the reign of Christ. *Pax Christi in regno Christi.*

When our Lord Jesus Christ raised marriage to the dignity of a sacrament under the New Covenant, he did nothing to change its natural character, the unity and indissolubility were written into marriage already at the level of nature. He made more luminous the necessity of the Faith to sustaining marriage and family life, which is why those who marry have to submit to the moral and natural law on the day they make their marriage vows, asking for the grace to perfect their union by grace, knowing exactly what their rights, duties and responsibilities are before God, each other and in society. The Apostle Paul is the mouthpiece when he reminds the married, in his characteristically energetic way, of the duties of spouses, parents, children and servants. In no uncertain terms he insists that these duties are nothing without a grasp of the fact that all authority is, in point of fact, divine in origin. He teaches us that we are duty bound to submit to the objective moral and natural law, giving to each what is his due, in a spirit of charity and love of one's neighbour, which offers us the best and most efficacious way of practising all the virtues. The family breaks down if there is no single point of reference in God any more. That rejection paves the way for competition, for a plurality of points of view about what duties and responsibilities actually are, it destroys the hierarchical structure of family life. Without the authority which God alone gives us to live, we then see this breakdown writ large in society as a whole: there is anarchy, which, in the manner of a sheet of lightning strikes and destroys without any warning, inflicting untold damage. Without the authority from God at work in family life children are at sea: instead of controlling their passions there is unbridled licence. Once this disease sets in, the prospects for educating disciplined and restrained citizens are weakened immeasurably.

Your task, dear ladies, is so great that it is impossible to imagine it will ever end. There is no such thing as instant relief to problems such as these. The remedies will require patience and self-sacrifice in inverse proportion to the speed with which the antagonist is able to destroy what you wish to construct and reconstruct. You will have to console yourselves with the thought that you are planting seeds which will only bear fruit at some unspecified moment in the future. Others may, indeed, be the lucky beneficiaries of your labours. But you will be able to take some credit for having saved the truth and the means of salvation. God will reward you throughout eternity with the crown of glory. But even in this world you may live to see and hear those who are perspicacious enough to know to give credit where credit is due. They will acknowledge your labours. Guided by the immortal teachings of the one, true Church, you will be sending out a courageous signal to those who have suffered anguish in the face of all these outrageous attacks on sacred life. Where others have failed, you will flourish by showing them the right royal road to happiness in this life and the next.

Your last congress in Rome was remarkable on account of the excellent spirit you brought to bear on your work. You all worked harmoniously towards the same goal. You were sincere in your devotion to Holy Mother Church and submitted to Her teachings without any mental reservation. You were free to talk to one another openly about what perplexed you; your discussions were open enough to permit private opinion where it was not in opposition to the teachings of the Church. At the same time you were united by that determination to ensure the common good. For these reasons I have no doubt that your work will flourish once more.

At this juncture I would like to congratulate your president, Mrs. Steenberghe, for all her work. She has worked ceaselessly for the great cause. She, together with her collaborators, has done all within her power to promote the international links between all the various leagues. She has watched over all the various initiatives, to protect them and guide them towards the common goal, thus ensuring unity throughout the apostolate.

I implore the blessing of the Blessed Virgin Mary upon all your works and labours, she the Mother of God, the Mediatrix of all Graces and the Co-Redemptrix. I beg of her to intercede with God, the Father, that our efforts bear fruit, and I rejoice in being able to cooperate in some small way, devoted as I am to the results which I know you wish to bring forth.

Posthumous Speech Prepared for the International League of Catholic Women, read out after the Cardinal's Death (*May 1930*)

It was four years ago that we had such memorable celebrations for the Jubilee Holy Year. You came to Rome on that auspicious occasion for the sixth conference of the international league of Catholic women. Those of you who took part will not have forgotten those beautiful and consoling gatherings or who were privileged to be amongst the audience. Your return to Rome for this the seventh conference brings back to life that same outpouring of joy since we have only just celebrated here in Rome the golden jubilee of the Sovereign Pontiff's priestly ordination. Our devotion to the august person of the pope is very special.

He too takes a very special paternal interest in your work and everything which affects the life of the League of Catholic Women, the range of your interests and concerns, the difficulties you have to cope with, your progress, and your success. I am sure all of this is very specially real to you today given that we are with him in such spirit over his priestly jubilee. I hope you will not consider it impertinent of me to speak to him on your behalf, offering him your filial devotion, love and gratitude as you embark upon your course.

You propose to take as your central concern the question of family morality whilst you are here in Rome, in particular to find the most efficacious remedies to counteract the deleterious effects of the world on same. Never before has the family been the object of such an insinuating campaign. It is the target of a plan. The idea is simple. Without being aware of being manipulated, the family is to be assimilated to the neo-paganism and sensuality of our day. This will ensure a given effect, calculated indifference in matters concerning religion. The evidence is everywhere before our eyes.

The plot hinges on family morality symbolically genuflecting to the new gods. Attacking the primordial stability of marriage, and its sacred and inviolable character as decreed by God is the requirement. Marriage is being transformed into a transient alliance at the mercy of transient human passions. It goes without saying that he who presumes to question God's laws or who overturns them with impunity runs the risk of provoking His just wrath. We will all be swept away by the effects of these acts of destruction. Marriage must remain indissoluble since it is the express desire according to the Divine Law that this be so, our Lord Jesus Christ having raised marriage to the dignity of a sacrament. Civil law is already treating the New Covenant with contempt. It comes as no surprise, then, to find that more and more people treat marriage with contempt and derision. Some of these people even claim to be Christian.

Look what is happening all around us, even as people feign to be unaware. It is impossible to be so. What motivates human action? The influence of nothing more than sheer, blind caprice, propelled by unregulated affection. This is everywhere in evidence. People contract alliances on the strength of nothing more than pure sentiment or on the strength of an aesthetic impulse, perhaps even to find an economic solution to their plight. These alliances are contracted in a rush, in defiance of other considerations. What, for instance, have they made of the fact that marriage is one of the seven sacraments? That the Church only bestows Her blessing on those who wish to marry with apprehension, given what is at stake? Have they given any serious thought to what their serious obligations and responsibilities are in this state of life, which is sacred?

And what happens to unions contracted for such frivolous

reasons? Even though they protest their desire for eternal love and stability and unity, everything about the way they live is superficial. What dominates is unbridled egoism, instead of that reciprocal spirit of self-sacrifice which makes marriage sacred. Blind passion caused the union to be born; it then sees to it that it is profaned. And when, the day after the wedding when everyone was convinced that this marriage looked so promising, the couple has to face the reality of sacrifice and duty which is characteristic of life together as man and wife, they are immediately frightened away, and seek ways of escaping all that God has created and sanctified for their own good. And thus we have the terrible prospect of ship-wreck in the home. The devastation of the family. The infallible logic of auto-destruction under the influence of passion and sin.

And what are we to make of the increasing number of mixed marriages? The Church has only ever permitted these to avoid a worse evil. In fact the Church has always deplored such marriages, and She deplores them with great bitterness, either in the case of those Catholics who are married to the heterodox or of those who are married to the unbaptized, who are not even Christian. Whilst no one can deny that occasionally such marriages are the efficient cause of the conversion of the non-Catholic party, with the grace of a family united by the Faith, in most cases this does not happen. Rather these cases are exceptional. In the majority of cases the faith of the Catholic party suffers. The Church watches with great sadness as She sees the harmful effects of these compromises and asks Herself what soul who really possesses the Faith would ever even countenance such a dangerous step? What seems to be more likely is that Catholics whose faith is already weak are drawn to non-Catholics, marry them, and the fruits of their lack of understanding, devotion or commitment thereafter become manifest. What is mixed marriage? It symbolizes lack of unity where it matters most, namely in the heart and at the heart of the home. Two souls live together who have wholly different conceptions of life and eternity; they are, therefore, not united in the Faith, but rather separated from one another by the Faith. People do everything in their power to cast a veil over these realities. But it is impossible to hide truth. It can be felt by those who have compassion in silence, when man's heart is at rest, registering what is impossible to deny. But this silence has another meaning. It is often the case that, for the sake of a false peace and in deference to the false virtue of human respect, that Catholics avoid their duties and do not speak out, professing the Faith in public as is their duty, denouncing error, defending revealed truth. Such couples have an unspoken pact. They avoid issues that are controversial, which is tantamount to a profession of neutrality on matters religious, and is the sin of religious indifferentism in practice. This comes at a price. It is difficult, painful and upsetting to be implicated in it, there is a sense of doing something wrong, there is shame at not resisting when one should. As they get older, the children are aware of these tensions. They are unsure. They do not know whom to follow. They get caught up in a downward spiral of nothing more than personal opinion. They are encouraged to discuss the problems they have witnessed in their own parents' marriages and make themselves judges of what is right or wrong, when, in fact, they have no authority so to do, and still less any real understanding of what is at stake. Families which are constructed around these problems prove unable to protect themselves against the infiltration of error, skepticism and rationalism. In practice, even when it comes to making a decision on how to educate the children, what threatens to undermine the Faith is nothing more than the fear of displeasing the other party, instead of being categorical and firm on points of doctrine. In the same way there is the same prevarication in respect of the sensual life. Instead of calling for restraint, all possible encouragement is given to the feverish pursuit of pleasure. In this kind of an atmosphere nothing is fixed and stable. Truth coexists with error. Truth becomes intimidated by error. She backs down, she is quiet. She is even wholly silent.

Because of precisely these tensions the bishops in Germany came to the assistance of the faithful in 1922 and 1923. They were painfully aware that so many souls were being lost through mixed marriages, not just the parents, but the children of such unions too; they were not unaware of the rise in the number of divorces; they could see that the risk of divorce in a mixed marriage was five times greater than in a marriage between two Catholics; that the children of such marriages fall naturally into Protestantism in general, in spite of the promises their parents make. By the third generation, the Catholic Faith has disappeared altogether. This is bitter indeed, and it is all the more appropriate for you to focus on these facts. It is our duty to do everything in our power to oppose these trends and these demands.

In considering all the various reasons for the decline of family life, you will, of course, be looking for practical solutions to help restore family life according to the model for family life, the Holy Family. Your concern is with a universal restoration, amongst the working classes, the farming communities, the intellectual milieux. Nothing could be more noble. Remember that, even if you do not have immediate success, you will at least be planting seeds which will bear fruit in the future. You will have helped to spread the benefits of the reign of our Lord, Jesus Christ.

I would like in this connection to draw your attention to two extremes, which you must avoid. The first is to cast something of a vague veil over the real causes of the trends in our societies on which we have already commented. It is our duty to know our adversary, to know his plans and to follow his plot. We must not allow ourselves to be merely displeased, aesthetically as it were, with some of the symptoms of decline. You must be specific. It is only by applying doctrine to the problems that we will be able to rise to the challenge of this specific mission and apostolate. If we are unaware or if we misread the real issues, then we are guilty of prejudicing the work which could do so much to save the souls of the next generation. We could, after all, be instrumental in shaping the opinion of the general public on what is going on, and that would be most useful. It is our duty to prevent any paralysis, and to inform the world of how God's laws are being subverted in our contemporary world. How can we rise to this task if we are not armed with facts and figures, as it were? How can we expect to have any effect if we are merely satisfied with a complaint, with a pose of moral repugnance, and little else? This is not real witness. This is mere human sadness and powerlessness.

The other extreme is, of course, to imply that what is happening is, in some sense, necessary and not sinful or evil per se. This would be to fall into the sin of human respect, the failure to speak the truth openly for the sake of upsetting the majority, and majority opinion. You are not to be intimidated by those who will inevitably try and cast you as old-fashioned, and out of touch. You are not to believe that the majority is leading the people to a triumphant victory, since that is obviously not the case. But that is how they see themselves. What we must protect is the deposit of the Faith, which comes to us from God. At times we will necessarily have to rest, whilst the tempest whips up feelings. But that is not to be confused with weakness in the fight itself. Your task of resistance requires more energy and courage than open warfare. But you must never allow mere expediency to suppress principles; you must separate error from truth. We must not betray our duty, which is to uphold Catholic doctrine, to resist the temptation to surrender, to protect true morality from its substitutes.

Here you must insist that pagan morality – which permits free reign to the passions – be fought in the name of the Christian tradition of self-control, of resistance to the perverse leanings of our fallen nature, doing everything in our power to reject the views of the reformers, who implied that nature could not be perfected, thus permitting all manner of sad perversity. We can never tolerate in silence the rehabilitation of evil. We can never permit by way of the false, pseudo-morality of modern science to believe that the shameless mockery of all things Christian is an unavoidable reality. We should always remember that civilizations go into irreversible decline once restraint is abandoned; that is the lesson of history. Nations collapse. Intellectual aberrations hold sway. Degrading corruption of public standards is everywhere in evidence. These are the inevitable consequences of abandoning God. The stinging criticism that we are retrograde is a badge of honour in this war, not a reason to succumb to the enemy. We, as members of the Church Militant, have a duty to fight for Christ, to spread the true gospel, to be his true disciples. Knowing this, we expect to have to confront the enemy, and to be mocked by the world. But whatever we do, if we wear the badge of our Divine Saviour, there is nothing we will not survive. It is a question of courage. We need not fear the anti-Christian and non-Christian forces. We remain silent when they seek to condemn us unjustly. At the same time we should be vigilant. There are many who are only hostile towards us because they do not understand what the Church teaches. They have no personal animosity towards us. These adversaries have no training in doctrine. They have simply been led astray, without having really considered what it is they claim to believe. They have been taken in by fashion, by novelty. Had they known the Wisdom of Holy Mother Church they would not have succumbed; had they realized that Holy Mother Church brings so much secular knowledge to bear in Her judgements, based on all Her awareness of the reality of human nature, they would not have rushed into the enemy camp. These are souls whom you must seek after. They will listen to you. They are able to be persuaded by the use of reason. They are not lost. All that is required is patience on your part. Teach them that the Magisterium of the Church is a living, teaching organ, which interprets the gospel for each new generation, indefectible, able to guide us through the maze of temptations which every new generation throws up. The Church does not have sterile, arid, abstract doctrines which bear no relation to reality; neither does She propose a philosophical system to be admired as an object. On the contrary. She has a living heart and soul, and a practical code which can guide each one of us individually, and society as a whole.

I am certain you will avoid the two extremes. Bring to bear that enlightened zeal for which you are justly known ... Dear Ladies, under the auspices of the Blessed Virgin Mary, our Heavenly Mother, may I ask you to begin your task. I implore the divine benediction for your proceedings with the whole of my heart.

Speech to Another Union for Women
(composed after March 1929)

Now that you have concluded your congress it is appropriate
for me to respond to the request put to me by your president
and members and talk to you very specifically about the
liturgy of the sacrament of marriage. As we are limited by
time constraints I propose not to tax your patience any further,
nor make any more demands on your tiredness after the last
few days, so I shall be as concise as possible. All I can do is
provide you with a brief sketch.

God in His omnipotence is always prompted to act in
accordance with His supreme Will. All He has to do is will,
and works body forth immediately. Man, by contrast, is a
weak and feeble creature by nature and is not able to produce
anything, given his nothingness. He is obliged to take recourse
to a whole range of different energies, many of which do not
come naturally to him, and to use all sorts of different instruments as means to achieve his ends. From this it follows that
God's majestic simplicity stands out as a shining light, making
all his magnificent works external signs of His infinite
grandeur. By contrast, man relies on seeing his works take
external form before him, being discernible to the human eye,
making a direct appeal to man's senses, as proof that his
efforts have resulted in acts and forms. As man is both body
and soul, his spiritual life and the gifts of grace constantly
demand real expression in space and time, otherwise he would
begin to languish and the effects of grace would be lost. Thus
it is that in the supernatural order, and specially in relation to
the sublime sacraments which make up our holy religion, we
find that unique combination, that ineffable grandeur, of
divine action embodied in forms of great simplicity. The
Church uses such forms as ways of explaining, illustrating and
giving external embellishment to truth, for the profit of man,
for whose benefit the sacraments were instituted in the first
place.

The first sacrament, one essential to salvation, is baptism,
and it clothes us in Christ, making us part of the royal priesthood, making us living members of the Mystical Body of

Christ. Divinely instituted, it is the visible sign of the regeneration of our immortal souls and it entails the mere sprinkling of a few drops of water on the forehead and the words we use to invoke the thrice adorable Holy Trinity.

Hidden beneath the veils, using nothing more than the most humble and vulnerable substances of a little bread and wine, God is able to operate the most marvelous miracle of His omnipotence, so that, night and day in our midst He is able to visit each one of us and to give each one of us both nourishment and support throughout our earthly life. And yet the ineffable sublimity of this mystery is contained in nothing more than a few very simple words, yet words which have a divine efficacy, words which our Lord said on the eve of his death, in the peace and quiet of the cenacle, with no additional adornment, in the presence of only the twelve apostles, giving us the greatest of all the sacraments, and the sacrifice of the New Law.

We notice the same combination of simplicity with efficacy in the case of the sacrament of holy marriage, which St Paul teaches us is held in great esteem because it is part of the mystery of Christ in the Church. When our Lord instituted the sacrament of holy marriage he recalled the creation of man, but he did not determine the precise nature of the form of the rite and did not even prescribe a new form. Once again we encounter the striking simplicity we have already noted, one which leaves us in no doubt of the nature and the essential terms of the contract, which is here elevated by him to the dignity of a sacrament and which will henceforth form the immutable and indispensable base of Christian society. Woman has been raised up from her fallen state and from her shame and given a new place in creation in the sanctuary of marriage, where she holds a place of honour with prerogatives that the divine plan has reserved specially for her from the very beginning and before the catastrophe of the original fall of Man.

Our Divine Master has bequeathed to the Church these incomparable treasures, like precious stones that one feels one should encase in order better to protect their beauty, and He has given to the Church the duty of surrounding all the great sacraments with all the appropriate solemnity, with prayers, with ceremonies of the kind which make quite clear to the faithful, in a visible manner, the very nature, the necessity, the efficacy and the holiness of all these institutions. In a word, he has given us the liturgy. We have the inspired language of the Church, a language which is eternal, one which is not always used just in very precise definitions of dogma, but which nonetheless contains doctrinal teachings from the Magisterium, and expressive of matters pertaining to the soul, to the extent that we all hold to the maxim *Lex orandi, lex credendi*. In point of fact the public prayer of the Church gives eloquent testimony of Her faith. As the matrimonial contract has become, for Christians, a sacrament, it will come as no surprise that it falls to the Church to regulate the necessary conditions for its validity and legitimacy as a pact, without prejudice to the legitimate and just part played by the civil authority in also laying down conditions of its own in terms of its understanding of marriage as a social contract. At the same time, we do not forget that municipal authorities or civil formalities are not capable of constituting the essence of marriage to true Catholics, and purely civil unions, no matter how solemn or legal their external forms, are illegitimate, null and without authority in the eyes of God. The limits of legitimate authority – religious and civil – have been inscribed in the recent Concordat signed between the Church and State.

It goes without saying that what is axiomatic in the marriage ceremony is that the contracting parties, who must be capable of marrying, give their consent freely, formally and deliberately, with no mental reservation in respect of the doctrines of the Faith relating to the sacrament. As marriage has been ordered to procreation, that means not intending to subvert the given ends and purposes of marriage. Consent at this level is an obligation, given the fact that marriage as a sacrament is worthy of being honoured in the way determined by the Church. If consent is not given in these terms, the marriage has not taken place, it is defective and non-existent in point of fact. Such defective consent is grounds for what the Church calls an annulment. For these reasons where annulments are granted the Church cannot be said to be annulling a true marriage, nor is she authorizing divorce. The contracting parties are themselves the ministers of the sacrament, which they administer to one another in front of a priest who is duly authorized to be their witness. They also do so in the presence of two other witnesses. These components are required by the Church who thereby bestows a public blessing on the promises exchanged by the couple.

These promises are framed by the liturgy of the marriage ceremony. The liturgy varies in the West and from the East; there are indeed legitimate cultural variations which have been formally approved by the Holy See but they all, nonetheless, testify to the high symbolism and significance of the solemn act of marriage.

What I will do now is simply restrict my comments to the Roman Rite and to the most well-known traditions here in the West. Unless there is a grave and manifest reason against following tradition, custom has it that the couple make their solemn vows in church, before the altar, indicating that their union is supposed to recall and repeat the union of Christ with His Church; that union is holy and its purpose is not just the propagation of the human race but to bring forth children for Holy Mother Church, co-heirs with the saints and children of God. By this we mean that parents should be raising up children to the supernatural life, to benefit from the Church and to participate in Her sacramental life in the love of God and Christ, not just give them natural life. For these reasons it is particularly regrettable that there are competing customs which undermine the proper clarity we need, if we are to understand marriage as a sacrament. That is to say the custom of not marrying in church, of marrying in a grand drawing-room, hired for the occasion, with all the trimmings of a society gathering, where the altar may not be distinguishable from any other table, since it is covered in flowers, rather resembling a display cabinet. Another profoundly regrettable custom is that of marrying late in the afternoon, with no Holy Sacrifice of the Mass and without Holy Communion. Do not hesitate to use your influence to bring to an end all these abuses which are so at variance with the true, Catholic spirit. Do what you can to enable those around you to better understand the importance of the nuptial Mass and the efficacy of the solemn blessing the Church bestows at the moment the couple agree to their mutual obligations and the very grave responsibility they have as they enter a new state of life, an account of which they must give to God at the Judgement.

With such admirable wisdom and clairvoyance and with Her maternal kindness, Holy Mother Church has never in fact opposed preserving certain rites and customs from Antiquity, as long as they were not in themselves reprehensible, nor incompatible with the Faith and Christian morality. Such customs have been adopted, it is true, but only once they have been transformed and sanctified by the Church, according to Her own prayers and customs. It is important to understand this, since the Church has been misunderstood on this point. Instead of seeing this process properly, as the way in which the Church bestows Her authority as a Church, we sometimes hear of the strange view that the Church has effectively simply co-opted pagan rites, adapting them to Her own customs, on which basis they allege that the liturgy owes its origin and character to pagan antiquity. According to this theory, what we know to be the august ceremony of the sacrament of marriage is no more than a repetition of profane customs with their purely pagan symbolism. Analogically, if we look at the obelisk at the center of the Piazza San Pietro, which is in fact a Christian monument because it is dominated by the glorious cross on which Christ died, symbolizing our redemption from sin, we would not be entitled to see in the obelisk anything more than a syncretic application of some arcane, Egyptian practice.

The victory of Christianity was celebrated by the erection of altars which were themselves built on the debris left behind by pagan temples, replacing the degrading and idolatrous sacrifices offered up there to the pagan deities. In doing so the Church was thus able to purify, cleanse and sanctify the very places which had been dedicated to false gods. That does not mean in any real sense that the Church went in search of the Faith amongst the pagans, nor that Her rites derived from pagan rites, since these were abrogated forever once Christianity triumphed. Neither does the persistence of some of the forms imply that pagan traditions have infiltrated their way into our new forms, but rather the reverse. Where they have survived they have already been transformed and made new by the Faith. Christians who are engaged to be married are thus required under pain of sin to celebrate their marriages in the Church and before the Church, a public body, and formerly, to make this point absolutely visible, those marriages were actually conducted in the open, in front of the façade of the church. Nowadays, young people are rather asked to enter the church and approach the sanctuary and to kneel down in front of the altar on the first step. This is their particular privilege as ministers of the sacrament and makes visible the holiness of the vows they are about to make.

The young woman is usually dressed in white and wears a crown of flowers on her head. According to tradition, the white dress symbolizes the modesty appropriate to a virginal soul and the innocence acquired in baptism when the soul was regenerated spiritually. She was robed thus in white at the beginning of her life when God's representative exhorted the new-born to keep free from stain of sin all through life that garment of grace, so that one day a new soul would be admitted to the Kingdom of Heaven. *Quam immaculatam perferas ante tribunal Domini Nostri Jesus Christi ut habeas vitam aeternam.* When a young woman wears a wreath of flowers in her hair – a custom which is widespread and entirely legitimate – our liturgists attach a certain significance to it, since it is indicative of another call, another exhortation, to a Christian woman to reign supreme in the home, with her husband, and to vanquish, with his assistance, all the assaults on her virtue and all the obstacles which she is likely to encounter on her way through life. Once at the altar rail the priest asks the couple to answer certain questions, separately, in order to obtain their formal and irrevocable consent to adhere to the sacrament and bond and vow of marriage. Once this consent has been vocalized the priest then invites them to join their hands and he then uses the prescribed formula: 'I pronounce you man and wife, in the name of the Father, the Son and the Holy Ghost'. From this point on, the marriage is valid.

This custom of joining the hands as an outward sign or

formal ratification of the pact, the convention or the contract and consequently of the agreement to live marriage according to the Church, is a long-standing one. It can be traced back to the depths of Antiquity and finds its rightful place in the liturgy of marriage. It also features in the Old Testament, in the Book of Tobias where we read of Raguel in the presence of the Angel of the Lord taking the right hand of his daughter and putting it into the right hand of Tobias, saying: 'The God of Abraham, the God of Isaac and the God of Jacob be with you, may he join you together, and fulfil his blessing in you' (Chapter 7, verse 15). It is because of this august tradition, no doubt, that we have the social convention, whereby a suitor asks for the hand of his bride from her father. The Roman Ritual then prescribes the blessing of the marriage ring, the ring symbolizing the vow of fidelity, *'annulus fidei'*, as Pope Nicholas I calls it. A great doctor of the Church, St Isidore of Seville, wrote that the husband gives the ring to his wife as a token of fidelity on his part, or better still, as a symbol of the union of their two hearts. Note here that there is only one nuptial ring properly speaking in our rite and reference is only made to one ring to be blessed. The husband takes it from the priest and passes it over the wife's finger. In doing this he is the first to make his vows and reiterates his promise, which the wife accepts according to her understanding, as both have reciprocal feelings. The man takes the initiative henceforth as the head of the family and the wife receives the ring as a symbol of this indissoluble union.

The promise of fidelity is by definition mutual, as without reciprocity it would not make any sense; it is equally obligatory by definition and is binding upon both in exactly the same way, all symbolized by the one ring. Christian morality is no different for a man than for a woman and the obligation to remain faithful to one's vows does not admit of variations. Where couples both exchange rings there may doubtlessly be some good reasons for the variation, but the liturgy itself only refers to the one ring. We are thus at liberty to draw the conclusion that the most minute details are rich in significance, as are the prayers and the ceremonial itself, all of which make up the celebration of the sacrament of marriage. At every step the intention of Holy Mother Church is to make literally clear that what is characteristic of the sacrament is its indissolubility as a marriage contract. What is at the apex of the marriage ceremony, thereafter, is the celebration of the nuptial Mass, which thereby underlines the solemnity of the vows. According to the wisdom of the Church the couple should desire to receive the sacraments at all times, and especially on this occasion, so it goes without saying that they will communicate on this day.

How beautiful the nuptial Mass is, so rich in signification, symbolism, so eloquent in its explication of doctrine, so rich in efficacy in its prayers and blessings and solemnity! The Introit of the Mass, for instance, tells us: 'The God of Israel join you together, and he be with you, who took pity on two only children; and now, Lord, make them bless thee more fully', an admirable and most sublime prayer. God must underpin each union; He alone is the prime mover; observing His laws is the duty of all married couples; it is only in His Divine Love that human love is able to embrace the demands of an inviolate Faith, giving us a rock-solid foundation.

After the Introit, follows the celebrated epistle of St Paul to the Ephesians which contains the law of married life. The Apostle provides us with a memorable list of the precise duties of wives and husbands, throwing resplendent light on the way marriage reflects the union of Christ with His Church. A society which shuns the authority of the Church necessarily leads to anarchy, so that the family is necessarily supposed to be the antidote, and the perfect example of humane government. And since society is nothing more than a further application of the laws of family and married life, it goes without saying that any anarchy in the family home necessarily engenders anarchy in society. Thus St Paul elaborates on the proper hierarchy of family life. The husband is the head of the family and must exercise his legitimate authority in such a way as to preserve and enhance mutual love, eschewing all lapses into tyranny, ensuring that his wife is always protected as the companion which she is; by his constant devotion to duty a husband governs and serves this royal family where a wife would never be able to go about her own duties with docility and confidence, if she herself did not humble herself before her superior, before her husband, whose duty is to protect her own prerogatives in the home which themselves guarantee tranquil domestic life.

In the Gospel of the nuptial Mass again we reflect on our Lord's ministry and how he instituted the sacrament of marriage. The Church repeats his words, and has done so again and again throughout the centuries, indeed will never stop reiterating Christ's warning to those who would have the temerity to legalize or justify divorce, and shroud such shameful talk in a series of specious arguments. What did he say? 'What God has joined, let no man rend asunder'.

The Holy Sacrifice of the Mass is thereafter offered up, in the customary fashion, and the sacred mysteries continue with the exception of one small change which happens after the *Oraison Dominicale*. The momentary interruption of the Mass is extraordinary in itself. We more typically come across such a pause in the rite of ordination of priests, when bishops are consecrated, when the holy oils are blessed, and when kings are crowned or when virgins are blessed. So this characteristic alone demonstrates the extent to which the Church holds marriage in such high esteem, and its sacred character. Our Lord is still on the altar under the Eucharistic veils, and thus in the presence of the Creator of Heaven and Earth, of our Divine Saviour, of the Judge of the Living and the Dead, the celebrant turns to the newlyweds and intones the sublime words in a loud voice, as a prayer offered up to God, one of an incomparable nobility. These last prayers, which are both ancient and sublime, are offered up principally for the wife, who is expected to imitate the saints, to be grave about her duty to remain modest, to protect her purity, to be knowledgeable about the doctrines of the Faith, to show her worthiness, in other words, as a wife, mother and protector of the peace in the home. All of this is nothing less than a canticle of praises and of vows, all of which throw into abundant relief the greatness of maternity in the Christian tradition, invoking upon the wife all of the abundance of divine blessings for her role in creation. A few minutes later the young couple approaches the communion rails and when they receive the Body and Blood of our Lord Jesus Christ they seal their union. This heavenly food will always be their strength in all the trials of married life as they walk hand in hand along the way to the gates of eternity. *O Sacramentum pietatis! O signum unitatis! O miraculum veritatis!*

Oh, if only all the young women whose hearts were set on marriage took their preparations for this new state of life seriously! Instead of which, what do we see? An excessive preoccupation, sometimes to the exclusion of all else, with externals, with the trimmings of what is no more than a society party, worrying about appearances, outfits, flowers, music, the honeymoon and the wedding present. What should they be doing? Meditating on the marriage as a sacrament, on the gravity of their new obligations as wives and mothers. What would happen if they stopped to consider seriously all these matters, and to reflect on centuries of wisdom about marriage, which the liturgy of the nuptial Mass contains? If souls took these matters seriously, think how many marriages could be saved, think how many off-hand unions could be avoided, think how many divorces would be hindered, think how many marriages would flourish, instead of disintegrating under the presence of worldly pressures and concerns, thereby inflicting so much damage on individuals and society, indeed, causing the destruction of Christian society as we know it.

I shall conclude this brief sketch of the nuptial Mass and its meaning by expressing my sincere wish that young people be better instructed in matters relating to marriage, so that, whilst we are surrounded by so many signs of decay, of the collapse of Christian morality, Christian marriage might yet flourish and regain its preeminent position in society in conformity with the doctrines taught by our Lord, Jesus Christ, His Church and our glorious Tradition.*

---

*This section is a new translation from the Italian by Harriet Murphy.

Conferences

Conferences to Novices

28 March 1921

The novices apply themselves to prayer and the study of the Constitutions. Afterwards they will go and spread the light of Christ because our Lord said to them in a special way 'You are the light of the world . . .' We are not the light merely for ourselves. We must reflect (like mirrors) the light of Him who is the true light, and in order to do that the mirrors must be pure and clear. The novices are applying themselves to this task by learning about our Lord so that they will be able to reflect Him in their lives . . .

17 January 1922

Have you ever noticed the words written around the cupola of St Peter's? 'Peter, do you love me more than these?' Well, you ought to apply these words to yourselves. You have been specially privileged by our Lord and therefore ought to love Him more than the others and to give him proof of this love by fulfilling His will. He reveals His will in the Rule, and in the smallest happenings of the day . . .

3 July 1922

The novices are now beginning their retreat. This is an important and decisive moment because they will never again in their lives have the leisure to spend time on themselves in quite this way. Under the impulsion of fervour people are sometimes tempted to make many resolutions. It is better to make a few only, making sure that these are sincere. A single virtue which is really practised will bring others in its train. Theology teaches us that the virtues are all related to one another. Each one of you will obviously make the resolutions which are most necessary in her own case. If I were asked for advice, I should tell you to base yourselves on a foundation of humility. Some exegetes go as far as to say that our Lord spoke about humility almost as though it were one of the sacraments. He said 'If you do not eat the flesh of the Son of Man and if you do not drink His blood, you will not have life in you'. And elsewhere 'If you do not become like little children, you will not enter into the kingdom of heaven'. He could have given us one or other of His virtues to imitate. He said, 'Learn of me who am meek and humble of heart'. This is, therefore, the chief lesson which our Lord wishes to teach us. It is an arduous task because pride, which is the strength of the weak, is so easy, whereas humility is so difficult, and in our actual epoch perhaps even more so than ever.

This virtue of humility seems to be so little understood. God, *as* God, would not practise humility, but used condescension towards us. He lowered Himself in order to come down to us . . . Let us try to descend, to abase ourselves in imitation of Him. Our Lord always strove to return to His divine Father. Let us try to imitate Him in this also; let us unite ourselves to God through prayer and recollection . . .

19 April 1926

Don't forget that our Lord knows each one of you individually and is concerned about each one as though she were the only person in the world. He does not behave like a king who on his accession to the throne throws handfuls of money to the crowd without knowing whom he is helping ... Nor is He like yourselves when you give alms to a poor man, not knowing at all who he is. No, Jesus knows you and gives you what is necessary. Put yourselves, therefore, under His gaze and into His heart, abandoning yourselves completely to Him ...

14 July 1927

You are going to take up the Cross. You should carry, not drag, this cross which you have so greatly desired. You will notice that it is a cross, not a crucifix. Jesus has left that space for you, for it is you yourselves who must be crucified.

Every morning, taking up the cross again, you ought at the same time to renew all the resolutions you made during your novitiate. These will help you to follow our Lord with complete detachment with regard to places, people, duties, and means ...

This cross needs a pedestal, and that should be your heart. And so that it may be worthy of this new Calvary, you must try to conform it ever more to the Heart of Jesus by imitating His virtue.

Then, as St Paul says, you will be virtuous even in this world because you will know how to rule yourselves and make progress daily in your union with our Lord ...

14 November 1929

You do not come to the novitiate to change your way of life
but to perfect it, seeking our Lord so that you may be ever
more united to Him. In order to achieve this you must remove
the obstacles, as the Prophet says, since they come from
ourselves. Sometimes it is a question of an apparently little
thing. A bubble of air can block water running in a pipe; likewise a small act of infidelity arrests the flow of grace in a soul
which, on account of it, is not completely given to God. You
must always work to get rid of these obstacles, without ever
giving way to discouragement. There may be occasions of
weakness but you must rise above them at once.

Our Lord sees our will to strive on, even when we fall.
When we pick ourselves up, we may not seem to have been
successful but actually we have made progress. There may be
apparent external successes but these do not count in God's
sight if we have not acted for Him. One essential is to work
for God, for His glory, and for souls ...

Conference in Honour of Our Blessed Lady

Gloriosa dicta sunt de te, Maria,
quia fecit tibi magna qui potens est
(The Feast of the Immaculate Conception)

Glorious things are said of Thee, O Mary, O Immaculate
Virgin, My Mother and My Queen, for He who is all-
powerful has accomplished marvels in Thee. It is the feast of
the *Virgo praedicanda*, of the Virgin most pure, whom the
Seas of old watched rising above the horizon of this world of
sin, in the shape of a spotless cloud, luminous as the bright-
est dawn, coming up from the desert, with Gabriel by her
side. She rose up in glittering robes, humble as a creature,
majestic as a Queen, bringing hope, pardon and joy to the sons
of men, who lay in the shadow of death, helpless to remove
the ban that blighted their existence and deprived them of the

bliss for which their hearts were yearning and must ever yearn, for they were made for God and cannot rest until they find Him: *'inquietum est cor meum donec requiescat in te'*.

It is the feast of our Most Amiable and Most Admirable Mother, *Mater Amabilis et Mater Admirabilis*, whose gifts and prerogatives deserve our loving praise: gifts and prerogatives that we can never cease to publish and proclaim to the ends of the earth, from generation to generation. For she has utilized them all to the utmost and fulfilled God's designs regarding her, as no other creature has ever done. By proclaiming her glory, we are doing honour to God in the most perfect work of His hands. From Him, her Creator, she has received all that she possesses, and when words of praise are on our lips, we are led to imitate her example to the glory of God, our Father, of the Eternal Word, Jesus her Son and our Redeemer, of the thrice Holy Spirit, her Spouse and the Paraclete of our souls.

But where shall we turn to find words with which to praise her adequately? How can we venture to sing the beauty of her exalted gifts when the Angels themselves are mute with admiration in her presence? The Patriarchs, in the majesty of their fatherhood, the Prophets in their far-reaching vision, the red-robed Martyrs in the matchless heroism of their sacrifice, the Virgins in the splendours of unsullied innocence, the Doctors of the Church in their abiding wisdom – all, yes, all, bow down before her as their Queen, whilst words die away on their lips, for even they are unable freely to express or to describe the marvels of God's power in Mary, the Virgin Mother. For she is the faultless mirror in which His perfections are reflected to the utmost degree possible in a finite being, in a creature of His hands.

Unable then to speak of her becomingly, let us ask God Himself to tell us of her glory. Prostrate in humble worship at the foot of the great White Throne let us listen to the great things that He says of her: *'Gloriosa dicta sunt de te, O Virgo Maria!'* The Voice of the Eternal Father is the first to reach our ear. Far back, before all ages, when time was not, in the unalterable tranquillity of God's eternal life, the Father speaks of Mary, the immaculate daughter of His love, or He lingered on the thought of her. He tells us that she was the object of His complacency and that His immortal gaze rested ineffably upon her with infinite joy. Yes, long before the world was made, before the earth was poised upon its axis, or the planets and the stars sped into space in the network of their orbits, before the waters of the ocean had been encompassed within their shores, or the hills had risen up to sing the glory of the Mother, long, long before, from all eternity, in the stillness of the triune life of God, Mary was there in the mind of the Eternal Father, in His thoughts and in His love: '*cuncta componens*'.

He looked upon His chosen daughter and adorned her with His gifts, building up in her the temple in which the only-begotten Son would dwell one day, in a manner worthy of His sanctity. We know that, speaking absolutely, no creature can be entirely worthy of Him, because, however perfect, it must always have the limitations of a finite being. But short of this, the omnipotence of the Father extended in her the possibility of perfection to its extreme limits and bestowed privileges upon Mary that are beyond our powers of conception. We read with wonder in Holy Writ of the marvelous splendour of the great temple that Solomon raised up on Sion, of the precious materials he gathered together from distant lands, of the skill of the workers he employed, and of the incalculable wealth lavished in its construction. And all this the son of David carried out under God's direction and blessing to build a sanctuary where His presence would be relatively felt and be the center of symbolical worship in the old Law. But after all, it was the work of men's hands and merely a material temple of stone. What then must be the grandeur of a living temple that God himself fashioned and adorned in the exercise of His almighty power, to prepare a home for the Incarnate Word and give a Mother on earth to His Divine Son? He denied her nothing that He could bestow on her, and His omnipotence could bestow everything that was not essentially excluded by the limitations of a created being. He enlightened her mind with a knowledge and insight of divine truth surpassing that of any inspired genius, for she was to be the Seat of Wisdom.

He raised her purity to such exalted heights of immaculate

radiancy by a form of redemption reserved to her alone, that it surpassed the spotless beauty of the angels, for she was to be the Mirror of Justice. He fortified her will in the strength of its docility and union with the Will of God, that she might become the Queen of all the Saints. He enriched her heart with the ineffable tenderness of a mother's perfect love, for He called her to be the Mother of Jesus and our Mother – the Mother of Divine Grace and the Repose of Sinners. 'How lovely are thy tabernacles, O Lord of Hosts', but of all thy tabernacles there is not one that can compare with this chosen sanctuary of thine, where thou hast so lavishly poured out the manifestations of thy power and the treasure of thy love. Verily, thou hast accomplished great things in Mary: *'fecit in ea magna qui potens est'*.

But there is a lesson to be learnt. Our hearts are also temples of God and the Eternal Father has created them with an exalted destiny. We are His tabernacles. He has blessed and purified them. He has enriched them with many gifts. Are we striving to keep our hearts pure and immaculate in order that they may be a fitting home for Him to dwell in? Are we utilizing our powers in His service or are we misusing them against His purpose and rendering ourselves unworthy of His presence and blessing?

In this wonderful work of the Creator in regard to Mary, the other two adorable Persons of the Blessed Trinity, the Eternal Word, by whom all things were made, and the Holy Spirit, the Sanctifier, acted together with the Eternal Father, for Faith teaches us that God is one and the three divine Persons, though distinct, are not separated or separable one from the other in the unity of their nature or in the operations of the Godhead. The Eternal Wisdom tells us of His delight in being with the children of men, *'deliciae meae esse cum filiis hominum'*. That delight He found primarily in Mary, whom He loved from all eternity as His Virgin Mother and extolled her accordingly before the choirs of angels in the heavenly courts. And the Holy Spirit, even in those eternal years before He breathed upon the waters of the new creation, was already sanctifying Mary and overshadowing her coming life (gifts of Holy Ghost). Thus did the Blessed Trinity think and speak of

Mary saying glorious things of her – '*gloriosa dicta sunt de te*'. But what God said of her on earth is not less glorious than what He says of her in the eternal years. Watch the Archangel Gabriel, the Messenger of God, speeding simply upon his way from the heights of heaven. He is not attracted nor delayed by the splendours of Imperial Rome, nor by the glamour of cultured Athens. As the ambassador of God, he is the bearer of a message, but his mission is not to the potentates of this poor world. Their wealth and fame, their great armies, their active trade, their vaunted schools of learning, he discards as undeserving of attention. He goes in quest of an unknown homestead in Galilee and to a humble maiden chosen by the Almighty to be the Mother of his only-begotten Son and hence to become the Queen of Angels and Saints. The message on Gabriel's lips is dictated by God Himself. The words he utters are the words of God. Listen to them as they linger in the air: their music will never cease to re-echo from generation to generation to the end of time: 'Hail, full of grace! The Lord is with thee. Blessed art thou among women'. O wondrous salutation, never before addressed to any creature before her, and never to be repeated! Wherever the Gospel of Jesus Christ shall be preached in the whole world, this praise of Mary shall be told for a memory of her. Hail, full of grace! Spiritual Vessel, that is to contain the Holy of Holies, more perfectly even in her immaculate heart than in her virginal bosom. Vessel of honour, worthy of all honours because honoured by God who has chosen her to be His Mother on earth. Hail, full of grace! See how her humility and self-abasement go on increasing in the reception of every added gift, rendering still wider her capacity for greater favours of God's love.

And then the Gospel tells us of her heroic sacrifice during the Passion, at the foot of the Cross, where she won the title of Queen of Martyrs. Hers was not a martyrdom of the senses; she never suffered any wound or injury in her body. Our Blessed Lord would not permit that His sinless Mother should be submitted to the indignity of shameless ill treatment at the hands of the vilest criminals, but the anguish of her soul was fierce beyond human expression and the sharpness of her distress exceeded all that the noblest heroes of the Faith have ever endured. Think of what our Lord suffered in the Garden of Olives at the sole prospect of His Passion and how the mental picture of His approaching torment causes His very blood to flow and prostrated Him to the earth in an excruciating agony. How terrible then must have been the pain that Mary endured who had the clear vision of the agonizing anguish in Gethsemane, the horror of the scourging and then actually followed in the footsteps of her Son along the dolourous way and witnessed the Crucifixion and the piercing of His Sacred Heart. She realized to the full all his cruel sufferings as only a Mother, and such a Mother, could realize them. And yet, she stood unshaken and majestic beneath the Cross, a queen indeed, the glorious Queen of Martyrs.

Moreover, it was there under the shadow of the tree, that the motherhood of Mary, the Second Eve, the Mother of the living, was solemnly extended to us her children and definitely received its final consecration from the Sacred Heart of our Saviour. '*Gloriosa dicta sunt de te, O Virgo Maria!*'

The Church takes up the hymn of praise. Century after century the voice of Her Fathers, of Her Doctors and Theologians is raised to extol the glories of Mary. The Psalms and antiphons of her liturgy describe in song her incomparable privileges, the power of her intercession, the beauty of her example, the wonders of her protection. 'Hail, O divine temple! Hail, throne of God!', exclaims St Ephrem of Syria. 'Hail, O house of God, glittering with divine splendour', writes St John Damascene.

God gave her an empire by linking the bestowal of His choicest blessings to her intercession. The Author of all grace came into the world through her. He had decreed that the Incarnation should be inseparable from her Maternity. It is almost as a consequence and development of this fundamental mystery that He should have wished Mary to be the chief instrument of His special gifts to the souls of men. This is the power, for He is the source of all light and of every gift. But He wishes that power to be preferably exercised through her and He has made intercession the principal channel of His greatest benefits. She herself is the greatest of them all, because by appealing to her we approach nearer and nearer unto Him. Such is her power of intercession that the Church does not hesitate to apply to her the very words that are primarily used in Holy Scripture to describe the marvels of divine Wisdom. Mary as the Mother of God and the Mother of men 'inspireth life into her children and protecteth them that seek after her'. The life she inspires is Jesus himself. 'He that loveth her loveth life', namely our Lord and God. 'They that hold her fast shall inherit life', that is to say the spirit of her Son, 'and withersoever she entereth God will give a blessing. They that serve her shall be the servants to the holy one ... and God loveth them that love her.' See how truly those words of the Holy Ghost have been fulfilled and are daily fulfilled in that power of her intercession! Read the lives of the saints and the faithful servants of God. You will find how they testify one and all to the graces they owe to Mary. Look at the innumerable shrines that have been erected in her name from the earliest times up to the present day, and see the records of the countless benefits, spiritual and temporal, obtained through the efficacy of her prayer.

Look into your own hearts and recall how often the invocation of her name has preserved you from sin in the hour of temptation, how in sorrow she has been a comfort, how she has brought you light amidst the darkness of doubts and fears; repentance after falls. In a word how she has led you to the feet of her Son: 'How close to God, how full of God, dear Mother must thou be, for still the more we know of God, the more we think of thee'.

The beauty of her example is no less worthy of our consideration than the power of her protection. She 'goes before us in the way of justice', to quote once more the words of the Holy Spirit. Justice, in the language of Scripture, denotes all virtues, full righteousness, sanctity, and Mary is the Mirror of Justice and the Seat of Wisdom. 'In the fear of the Lord is wisdom and discipline and that which is agreeable to him is faith and meekness'. Faith, the homage of the mind, meekness the homage of the will. Mary's faith was heroic. In the darkest hour of her martyrdom, of her desolation 'she kept his words in her heart' and believed with ever-increasing steadfastness. Mary's submission to every commandment of God and her eagerness to correspond to every inspiration and desire from above increased her merit by leaps and bounds: 'she rejoiced in the living God' (Psalm 83). The *'fiat'* she uttered in response to Gabriel's salutation, characterized her whole life. It sums up all her virtue. She renewed it before holy Simeon in the Temple on the morning of the Presentation, she repeated it when Jesus was lost in Jerusalem, she lived on it during the thirty years of poverty and labour in Nazareth. It never left her lips along the way to Calvary and the angels heard it again at the foot of the Cross and in the silent tomb where she laid the wounded body of her crucified son in the evening of the first Good Friday.

She goes 'before us in the way of justice'. It is for us to follow in her footsteps. We have not her graces, but we have our own. They are many, they are great, and they are constantly lavished upon us by God's infinite bounty. He has called us to the Faith, He has regenerated us by His most Precious Blood. He has given us his commandments to guide us, His sacraments to sustain and sanctify us. He has made us children of His Church and has destined us to eternal glory, if only we will follow the path He has laid out for us and which He Himself has trod. Mary is there to protect us and she is our Mother. Her example is before us to encourage us. Let us ever utilize our graces as she utilized hers. Let us accomplish our duties faithfully for God's glory and the daily burden will not only be lightened but will bring its own reward. 'The judgements of the Lord are true ... and in keeping them there is a great reward' (Psalm 18). Confiding in her intercession we can bear our cross.

Glorious things are said of her in heaven and on earth, and glorious things will be said of us before the throne of God. They will be said by Mary. Our merit will be in the measure of our efforts. In our very weakness we can shine forth as 'mirrors of justice' if we seek God's will in all things, and serve Him by the purity of our lives, with perseverance to the end.

Conference on the Blessed Sacrament

*All good things came to me together with her and
innumerable riches through her hands.*
(Wisdom 7:11)

It must have often struck you, dear Brethren in Jesus Christ, when reading in the Old Testament the detailed account of the life of the chosen people during the forty years they spent in the desert and their subsequent sojourn in the land of promise, what an important part the Ark plays at every step of their eventful history. Its presence was their greatest safeguard and a sign of God's constant protection; its loss was inevitably followed by some terrible disaster to Israel, negligence or want of respect towards this token of divine friendship was punished in many cases with instant death. If it came to fall into the hands of God's enemies, it spread consternation in their ranks. For it was not to be a source of blessing for them, but to the people of Israel, who were taught to appreciate this great gift better through its momentary withdrawal.

The chosen people of God today are all the true followers of Christ, all those who believe His doctrine, obey His law, and belong to His Church. It is therefore a natural consequence of God's wise Providence that there should exist in our midst something equivalent and yet more perfect than the Ark; for the principal institutions in the Old Law were but a figure or preparation of what was to take place in the New, and if we had no other reason, this visible sign of His friendship to His chosen people before the coming of the Messiah, He cannot fail to bestow a corresponding gift of still higher value on us who are in a special manner the children of His love. And in truth He has done so, surpassing in His infinite generosity all that we could hope for. He is not content to institute a sign, however exalted, which would manifest His condescension and tell us by its presence or its absence whether we are deserving of His mercy or His wrath. He must come Himself in the Blessed Eucharist and abide with us, not amidst the awe and terror that surrounded the inner precincts of the Temple, but in the humblest and most attractive manner. The Ark contained the Tables of the Law and Aaron's rod, the manna of the desert and the loaves of propitiation. But beneath the Eucharistic veils we have more than that, for there is the very author of the Law, the Eternal priest, the bread that came down from heaven and gives life to the world. When this thrice holy sacrament is in our midst all goes well; when we have it not and deprive ourselves of this heavenly food we must gradually lose all strength and die. If we show disrespect for this precious gift or despise it in sacrilegious communion we are punished by the severity of God's judgements, even in this world. The unbelievers and declared enemies of Christ's Church into whose hands this Sacrament has fallen have often suffered some terrible visitation of God's wrath as the Philistines of old when in the presence of the Ark. But to follow the line of Wisdom I set forth when first I addressed you, it is not of the punishments that the Blessed Eucharist may call down upon us of which I have to speak today; but rather of the fruits and blessing that we derive from the Holy Eucharist if, believing in it with a firm faith and understanding the obligations it imposes upon us, we approach and receive it with proper dispositions. By God's grace we shall see that the bountiful effects of the Sacrament are not only to be found in individual souls but are especially visible in society. And extending their heavenly influence on every station and position in life they bless and sanctify whatever intercourse can and should exist between man and man.

When God by a single word called the universe forth from nothingness, His design and final object was none other than that the work of His hands should be a living and perpetual hymn of praise and gratitude before the throne of His awful majesty. Man was constituted the Supreme High Priest of this glorious temple and the Lord of all. Creatures were to pay tribute to God and cooperate with Him in order that, as His representatives and intermediaries, they could render homage to the all-wise and bountiful Creator. Eternal Love gave life to creatures, and man, alone capable in the material world of understanding and of love, was to give back to God by an act of adoration the being he had received and that which had been bestowed on the creatures at his feet. But sin destroyed this admirable harmony and broke the link that united the Creator to His work. It was in order to restore all things and by sanctifying grace to lead fallen humanity back to God and still greater perfection, that the Incarnate Word has dwelt amongst us. For this purpose also, as we have seen and with a view to making our resurrection from sin more complete, this bountiful Saviour places Himself beneath the species of bread and wine, the noblest of the earth's fruits, and gives Himself by this means to man as food. He reestablishes that original harmony, for as St Paul describes it, 'being consummated He became to all that obey Him the cause of eternal salvation' (Hebrews 5:9).

Man's perfection stands in proportion to his resemblance with God, who alone is essentially holy, essentially pure, essentially good (perfect in a word). The more man resembles Him, the more perfect will he be. It is evident however that this gradual process of his sanctification can only be brought about by living with God and constantly communicating with Him. But the Eucharist is precisely the continual dwelling of our Lord with us and in us and we must therefore conclude that the nearer and the more often we approach the Sacrament, the nearer we shall approach God, the more intimately shall we participate in His life, in His thoughts, in His desires, in His actions and therefore the more shall we resemble Him and the greater will be our perfection. When we speak of morality we mean the annihilating of all that degrades and lowers man: we mean the systematic rejecting of everything that takes us from God our first principle and our ultimate end, we mean in fine the aspiration of our being towards what is alone worthy of its sublime dignity. Now the Eucharist is the most complete and perfect actuation of these effects in those who really make it the food of their souls, and earnestly desire to imitate in all its parts the inner life of their divine Master.

For in the first place the Blessed Sacrament, like a glorious luminary in the spiritual firmament, inundates our intelligences with a light to see and understand the things of God, so often unknown to those who are engrossed with worldly pleasures and material interests. Simple and humble souls frequently acquire in this Eucharist a penetrating and mature judgement that nature has not given them. Scientific men find a help there and a safe-guard against that danger overhanging some powerful minds, that of attributing to themselves or to creatures what belongs to their Creator; for at the foot of the altar they realize more perfectly that true science must go hand in hand with faith because they both come from God, and that when our limited knowledge seems to make them clash we must call our science to task but not our faith. To all in fact the Eucharist shows where duty lies and aids and strengthens us to act up to it. Man is being constantly dragged away from God by his rebellious nature and by the world that seeks to flatter his passions: to break with the allurements of the one and resist the inclinations of the other in order to tend to God, no human power can suffice, but the Blessed Sacrament brings us a strength which is all divine and frees us from the tyranny of our enemies, for like St Paul we too can do all things in Him who strengthens us.

This complete union of the body and soul of our Lord Jesus Christ with the body and soul of man awakens in every indi-vidual a full and holy consciousness of his sublime calling. 'Christians, acknowledge thy dignity,' writes St Leo, 'and having become partaker in the divine nature return not by a degenerate life to thy former deprivation.' Pride is based on falsehood, but this self-esteem which comes from God has its foundation in humility, for it begins by opening our eyes to the fact that we owe everything to our Blessed Saviour and that by His grace and His mercy we are what we are: it was what St Paul meant when he saw that God's grace had not been void in him: I have laboured more abundantly than all they, who am not worthy to be called an Apostle, yet not I but the grace of God with me. This holy consciousness of our dignity that the Eucharist produces in our hearts makes us understand and acknowledge that our immortal souls are something more precious than the world with all its riches, its honours and its joys. When endowed with this supernatural power we can afford to forfeit the esteem of men and welcome the contempt we suffer at their hands for God's sake.

Brethren, we must have met some of these souls who, after possessing all that wealth, talent, social and domestic happiness could bestow upon them, have been cast into poverty by some sudden disaster or into sorrow and shame by the loss or the sin of those who lived beside them. And yet they have bravely stood on the ruins of the past and taking up their cross with joy, they have breathed courage into the hearts of those who had ceased to hope. Ask them where they found that strength that others have sought in vain! They will tell you that in the hour of need they had turned to Jesus in the Blessed Sacrament and that their trust had not been misplaced, 'for all good things had come to them with Him and innumerable riches through His hands'. Ask of those souls whose peaceful and angelic life you perhaps have often envied, ask them how it is their possessions have lost all hold upon them, how it is they are not led away by the love of earthly things and that they pass unscathed where others so often fall and they will answer you that the Eucharist is the source of all their bliss. When passions and temptations, illness and sorrow had gathered threatening storms around them, they turned to Him, Who in the tabernacle as of yore in Peter's bark had seemed to sleep and He had heard their cry and with one word had given them back the peace that they had lost. They will tell you that they have found in Him a Master who taught them how false and shallow the world is, a Father who is anxious to forgive and slow to punish, a brother and a friend who has shown them how to live His life, to hate what He hates, to love what He loves, to seek out God's will in all things and to sacrifice their own. Since then they have looked at things in their true light: with their eyes fixed on the Eternal Years, they have found in fact in the Blessed Eucharist the way and the truth and the life and with St Paul they have long since been able to feel sure 'that neither death nor life, nor angels nor principalities nor powers, nor things present nor things to come ... nor height nor depth nor any other creature shall be able to separate them from the love of God, which is in Christ Jesus, our Lord'. Such are, dear Brethren, together with the remission of venial sin and diminution of the penalties due for our faults some of the principal fruits produced by the Blessed Sacrament in the individual soul.

But we must go a step further and see how this lifegiving influence of the Eucharist can shed its merciful light over our social relations and how it actually does so amongst those who really make it their spiritual food. Social order and social happiness must necessarily be the result of the virtues and consequent happiness of the individuals that make up the community. We have seen that the beneficial effects of the Eucharist enable each one of us to lead a life of spotless innocence and ever-increasing merit. We must thence conclude that if by uninterrupted union with the Blessed Sacrament we were all endowed with light to act with prudence, and strength to be constant and persevering in the practice of individual duty, society composed of such elements would indeed be a model of a perfect community and the home of untroubled peace. Still, there do exist certain virtues that occupy a special place in social life and which are necessary in order to sanctify the relations of one individual to the other and unite us all that we may be the better enabled to face the dangers and difficulties of the journey towards eternal happiness.

Now these social virtues, dear Brethren, are brought about, maintained and strengthened by the presence of the Blessed Eucharist in our midst. One of the first fruits of this heavenly food in the souls of those who partake of it is the spirit of charity, and without it true social happiness is a dream. Selfishness was a necessary sequel of original sin and ever since that day man has had to combat in his fallen nature an enduring tendency to seek himself, his own comfort, his own advantage at the expense of his fellow creatures. Divine charity, on the contrary, taught and practised even unto death by our Lord Jesus Christ is indeed as St Paul puts it, kind and envieth not, is not ambitious, seeketh not her own, is not provoked to anger, beareth all things, believeth all things, hopeth all things, endureth all things and never falls away (I Cor. 13:4). It makes us look upon every human creature as the member of one great family and inspires us to divide with others the material and intellectual goods that may have fallen to our share. How this spirit of charity cannot be completely understood or fully practised where the Eucharist is unknown! A sentiment of pity for a being that suffers is almost inseparable from human nature: you will find it recorded in pagan history and discover traces of it even amongst the uncivilized savage tribes, but that is not Christian or Catholic charity, since that alone makes man love for God's sake and see Him in his fellow creatures. And now that money and pleasure have become the ideal of almost every class in society, how little real charity exists! I desire not to speak disparagingly of those good works performed in the name of philanthropy, you will let me call it, Christian charity paganized – it is all very well in its way – but poor and suffering souls need something more than hard coins, they too must be taught to love their fellow creatures with that charity that envieth not and is not provoked to anger (I Cor. 13), they must feel a heart in the hand that gives. If that charity is wanting you may throw millions to the multitudes; they will not and cannot be satisfied. But let all partake of this wondrous food that God's love has prepared for us and you will see how soon selfishness and envy would give place to charity and peace! If rich and poor, employers and employed, masters and servants were often to kneel side by side at this dinner banquet, they would rise from it hand in hand and united by a bond that would never be severed, the bond of the love of God. The wealthy would see that it is their glorious privilege to imitate their Saviour in His Eucharistic life and, setting aside all sensual pleasures, they would give not only what they have, but give themselves and spend their energies, talents and activity in the service of those around them. The poor would learn from that sweet Sacrament, that their poverty is no shame but the glorious livery of a suffering Master who has proclaimed them blessed: they would know that they have nothing to envy in those whom God has placed above them in this world, for theirs is the Kingdom of Heaven. Ah, Brethren, if, in our great cities, in those hovels of the poor, the home of misery and of sin, the Eucharist were known and loved, if those unfortunate souls could realize that in a street close by their Lord and God was present, living in poverty and forgotten as they are and yet able and ready to help them at any hour, anxious to forgive the past and lead them to a land where 'God shall wipe away all tears from their eyes and death shall be no more, nor mourning, nor crying, for the former things have passed away', if this could take place there would be a bright side to the picture after all, the so-called social question would be forever solved.

Yet that is not all. Side by side with the spirit of charity, the Blessed Eucharist bestows upon society its sister virtue, the spirit of sacrifice which is the basis of Christian life. 'For unto you it is given,' says the Apostle, 'for Christ not only to believe in Him but also to suffer for Him' (Phil. 1:29). To wish to imitate our Lord and refuse the Cross is folly, it must be our daily companion and if we only embrace it generously it is the key to Heaven. It may come to us in the unwelcome garb of everyday duty and hidden trials. The poor man at his work, the student at his books, fathers and mothers with their children, young and old in a battle with their passions and temptations, the sick on their bed of suffering, those cast down in sorrow or bereavement, whatever our station in life may require we all have something to suffer, we have a sacrifice to offer. And who will teach us to make that offering generously for the glory of God and the love of others? Where shall we learn to read in the great book of God's Providence and see in every little circumstance of our lives a messenger of His Justice or of His mercy, to pass over and forget the faults of others, to be patient with them and patient with ourselves, to make in fact our family and social gatherings the center of heavenly peace? Where indeed if not in that great Sacrament of Divine Love the Blessed Eucharist? There we shall be shown not only how to bear our crosses but how to love them. Here it was that St Teresa was taught to wish to die rather than cease to suffer. Cecilia and Agnes, Ignatius and Sebastian, and all the virginal holocausts of the Coliseum found in that food the strength to face undaunted the cruelty of their enemies. It sustained the courage of Fisher and of More, of Margaret and of Campion and of all those heroic warriors of the Church and some of England's noblest sons in Tyburn and on Tower Hill. The Blessed Sacrament is today the hope and joy of those who go to shed their blood in distant lands for the propagation of the Faith. Damian amongst the lepers, the Sister of Charity in the drudgery of her hidden apostolate, chaste souls amidst the austerity of the cloister, Catholic laymen in their generous battle in word and writing against the enemies of God's cause, all are vivified, strengthened and urged on to the great sacrifice of themselves by partaking of that Sacrament where Christ is immolated for us. Death itself bows down before it, for it extends its merciful effects before the tomb. At the divine banquet we can meet the souls of those dear ones who have gone before us, for the Lord whom we receive in our breasts is the same on whom they gaze. He is their joy if in Heaven, their hope if in Purgatory as He is ours in this place of exile and in Him we can all be one. Heavenly union indeed, glorious Communion of the Saints where the poor are made rich, the widow and the orphan are comforted, the sick and dying forget the past in this assurance of an eternal future.

Brethren, is it not true then to say that the Eucharist is the life of God's Church and the centre of His worship? As our souls sustain our bodies and, animating them, preserve them from corruption and give them vigour and energy, so does the Eucharist in the great universe of created things, make the Church a society different from every other society, because they will die, but She must ever live. As the air, which is spread about everywhere in creatures and fills the breast of every living creature, seems to bind us all together, so is the Blessed Sacrament all over the world; its influence is felt everywhere, its very essence recapitulates the sum total of Revelation, devotion to it comprises all other devotions without excluding any, it is the ultimate explanation of our hierarchy, of our monasteries, of our chapels and of our altars, the evangelical counsels take root there, the Sovereign Pontiff like the humblest of Christ's followers must go to it for comfort and for help. These are the fruits and blessings we derive from the Eucharist. Can we ever appreciate them as we might, for indeed 'all good things have come to us together with it and innumerable riches through its hands'?

Make it then the centre of your lives and the constant object of your worship. Your first thoughts in the morning and your last before going to bed should be turned to the tabernacle where your Saviour is dwelling and praying for you. In the midst of your occupations however necessary and important they may be, in the heat of lawful pleasure and amusement, never lose sight of Him who all the while is watching you from the Altar throne. Keep a corner in your hearts free from the spirit of the world where, as in a hidden sanctuary, you can escape from the outside world to adore your Lord and God. If you are thus faithful to Him in life, He will not abandon you at the hour of your passage hence. In that dread journey Jesus will accompany you and at that last communion more beautiful even than the one when yet a child you first received Him in your soul, you will hear the merciful sentence: 'Come ye, blessed of my Father, receive ye the Kingdom prepared for you from the foundation of the world'. At your approach, the eternal gates will be lifted up, for you will enter with the King of Glory. The Eucharistic veils will cease to hide their Lord and you will see Him face to face as the angels do in the joys of a glorious eternity, a blessing that I wish you all in the name of the Father and of the Son and of the Holy Ghost. Amen.

Prayer for the Beatification of the Servant of God

Most Holy Redeemer, and Lord Jesus Christ, Who didst vouchsafe to endow Thy servant Cardinal Merry del Val with choicest gifts so that from the height of his dignity should shine the priestly virtues of charity, of zeal for the salvation of souls and of Christian mortification, we beseech Thee, if it be in conformity with Thy Holy Will that Thou wouldst glorify him on earth by granting through his intercession the favour ... that we fervently implore of Thy most Sacred Heart, to Thy glory and to the glory of the Mother of Sorrows whom he so tenderly loved and honoured on earth.

One Our Father, seven Hail Marys, One Creed

Please report favours received through the intercession of the Servant of God to:

Mgr Tomás-Amable Díez Olano
Postulator of the Cause of Cardinal Merry del Val
Pontifical Spanish College
Via di Torre Rossa 2
00165 Rome
Italy

www.ingramcontent.com/pod-product-compliance
Lightning Source LLC
Chambersburg PA
CBHW031855090426

42741CB00005B/509